D1245423

WISDOM the principal thing

WISDOM,
the principal thing

STUDIES IN PROVERBS

By
Kenneth L. Jensen

PACIFIC MERIDIAN PUBLISHING CO.
13540 - 39th AVENUE N.E.
SEATTLE, WASHINGTON 98125

To my wife, Dorothy, who constantly keeps me in
balance

To my spiritual father in the Lord, William (Bud)
Evans, who was God's faithful tool to evangelize
me.

To two congregations I have served,
First Baptist Church of Falls City, Nebraska
Sunset Hill Baptist Church, Seattle
who have responded to Bible doctrine so
enthusiastically.

Acknowledgments

This is to express my indebtedness to my *didaskalos* (Greek for teacher), Rev. R. B. Thieme, Jr., Pastor of the Berachah Church, Houston, Texas. Of all those men who have advanced my knowledge factor, he stands alone as the master of all. His untiring efforts to search out truth from Holy Scripture keeps us mindful that the pastor-teacher must never become lazy or apathetic to study. Much of the content of this book owes its existence to my teacher, one of the leading Bible expositors of modern times.

In addition, an expression of thanks for their help in the formulation of this endeavor is given to the following:

Donald W. Patten	in an editing capacity
Lois B. Odell	in an assistant editing capacity
Emma Hale	in technical organization
Donald J. Gerards	in artwork preparation
Christine Lechelt	in transcript typing
Joan Taylor	in transcript typing

Foreword
Wisdom the principal thing

There are a number of young men who are functioning as Pastors in our generation, and who are positive
to Bible Doctrine. These men have the vision of an
exegetical, categorical approach in teaching the Word
of God. They have parted from the traditional homileti-
cal approach which cannot and does not fulfill the
principle of feeding the flock of God.

Ken Jensen, the author of this book, is one of these
young men, because he has chosen the Bible way in
regards to communicating Doctrine. I heartily recom-
mend this book to you. Ken has been the recipient of the
teaching ministry of Berachah Church and has been
academically honest in accreditation.

As a friend and fellow Pastor, I consider it a privilege
to encourage the up and coming generation to live by
the Word and for the Word and through the Word of
God. May you enjoy this volume as much as the author
enjoyed writing it.

R. B. Thieme, Jr.
Pastor, Berachah Church
Houston, Texas

Introduction

WISDOM the principal thing is based on a selection of sermons from Proverbs by Pastor Jensen. They were given on consecutive Sunday nights during the years 1969 and 1970 at Sunset Hill Baptist Church, Seattle. The title of this book, like the contents, suggests the practicality, the scope and the vitality of Proverbs' short, terse but colorful teachings.

This material is but a selection of that which was presented. As this book finds success in the market, a sequel will be under consideration. This work mines some of the spiritual wealth of Proverbs, a book unique in the scriptures and yet so similar to the parables of our Lord.

Donald W. Patten
January 1971

Contents

List of Diagrams

CHAPTER I

The Three Thrusts Of Proverbs

Wisdom is the principal thing;
Therefore get wisdom.
And with all thy getting, get understanding.

Exhalt her, and she shall promote thee:
She shall bring thee to honour,
When thou dost embrace her.
Proverbs 4:7-8

THE INTAKE OF PHYSICAL FOOD fulfills several diverse functions within the human body. Similarly, the soul-food contained in Proverbs serves several purposes when it is digested by the human soul. The general functions of the proverbs are categorized in what we entitle the Three Thrusts of Proverbs. Briefly defined, the three thrusts are as follows:

Thrust 1 — Emphasis: MENTAL ATTITUDE.
Proverbs gives divine viewpoint* which

*Throughout the body of this work, asterisks will indicate terms that have been used in a particular way by this author and therefore are defined in the Glossary.

helps to develop the Mind of Christ, in the
believer.

Thrust 2 — Emphasis: DIVINE NORMS AND
STANDARDS
Proverbs' divine viewpoint develops within
the believer discernment and objectivity, the
knowledge of right from wrong, within the
believer.

Thrust 3 — Emphasis: OVERT ACTIVITY.
Proverbs gives divine viewpoint to establish
divine norms and standards which govern
the overt activities of the believer, activities
which should please God and edify the human
race.

The three categories just described are condensed down and
synthesized from the whole book of Proverbs, but these three
emphases can be seen most clearly in one passage, Proverbs 11:1-3.
Once they are known categorically, it will be easy to recognize
how implicit these principles are in other sections of Proverbs.
The three thrusts of Proverbs have been listed in what we consider
to be their order of importance, although they do not appear in
that precise order in Chapter 11 of Proverbs.

When pride cometh, then *cometh shame;* *But with the lowly is wisdom.* *Proverbs 11:2*	Thrust 1 Mental Attitude

The integrity of the upright
  Shall guide them:
But the perverseness of trans-
  gressors shall destroy them.
Proverbs 11:3
	Thrust 2 Divine Norms
	and Standards

A false balance is abomination *to the Lord:* *But a just weight is his delight.* *Proverbs 11:1*	Thrust 3 Overt Activity

Thrust 1: Mental Attitude

The aim of Thrust 1 is to create or develop within the believer the Mind of Christ, a godly Mental Attitude. I Corinthians 2:16 and John 1:1 teach us that the Bible is the Mind of Christ, and Philippians 2:5 gives us an order, "Let this *mind* be in you which was also in Christ Jesus." The application of Thrust 1 is to learn *gnosis*[1] (Greek for *knowledge,* in this case knowledge of the Bible), and then store it in our "hearts" as *epignosis* (Greek for *full knowledge, wisdom,* or *knowledge applied*).

Proverbs, as will be discovered shortly, repeatedly chastises mankind for mental attitude sins, those kinds of sins which are not always evident to others, but which shatter our fellowship with God, since He looks on our hearts.

Mere religionists adhere to a strict code of legalism[2]. Legalism is, at its best, just a superficiality, a substitute for Christianity. God is primarily looking for believers who can and will control their thought patterns first. Pride is the chief perverter of the thought pattern. It is also the chief initiator of chain-sinning, which includes such secondary iniquities as envy, hatred, jealousy, vindictiveness, and inevitably, gossip and maligning (sins of the tongue). The first half of Proverbs 11:2 might be paraphrased to read, "When pride comes, then comes dishonor to both God and the believer." Dishonor comes to God when a believer assumes the lie of self-sufficiency apart from God's grace. Dishonor comes to the believer because pride destroys the true modus operandi* for the Christian Life, leaving the believer to fail miserably at grace living. Believers who gossip one moment, and the next moment claim Christ as their Lord only discredit Him. They make a mockery of their prime purpose in life, which is glorifying God.

The Gospels waste very little time telling us about the details of Christ's overt behavior. For instance, they do not tell us how

---

[1]The sources for all Greek and Hebrew words used throughout this work are listed in the bibliography on page 164.

[2]"I don't smoke nor drink nor chew, and I don't run with the boys who do," is an American colloquialism which mocks the superficiality of legalism. See Glossary for a more detailed definition of legalism.

much wine He drank at the marriage at Cana. Nor do they tell
us how low He hung His head to show humility. What the Gospels
do tell us are the words He spoke. The tongue will inevitably reveal
the mind of a speaker. The Mind of Christ exhibited only grace,
never mental attitude sin.

"Wisdom," says line 2 of this proverb, "lies with the *lowly*."
Does this mean that a successful man cannot be wise? Not at all!
"Lowly" means humble, and God always recognizes humility,
as is seen in I Peter 5:5,

> *... be clothed with humility, For God resisteth the proud,*
> *and giveth grace to the humble.*

When Peter said "giveth grace," he meant "blesses." This verse
and the one following teaches a principle that seems contradictory
in human terms, that is, a man becomes successful by being lowly.
God resists the proud by turning their pride to shame and dishonor; He makes their hypocrisy apparent. Soon everyone laughs
at them behind their backs and eventually, even to their faces.
God exalts the humble and causes them to succeed in overt forms
of life, as well as in inner progress in spiritual growth.

Humility, God-consciousness and God-thankfulness, rather than
pride, exemplifies the Mind of Christ. One might ask how a man
could be called humble who once said,

> *I am the way, the truth and the life; no man cometh unto*
> *the Father, but by me.*
> *John 14:6*

If this seems confusing, it is only because of a misunderstanding
of the word HUMBLE. Humility goes hand-in-hand with honesty.
Humility recognizes one's achievements as well as one's failures.
It recognizes that God leads and motivates. If a humble Christian
recognizes that he has been successful in some area, he does not
immediately assume that he is superior to his fellow believers;
he realizes that what he is or is not is only by the grace of God,
(See I Corinthians 15:10). He thanks the Lord for the accomplish-
ment(s), forgets it and moves on to the next phase of his life
(Philippians 3:13, 14). He may realize his success or failure in
achieving godly objectives, but he never compares himself with
others. Others do not comprise a standard; God's leading does.

Pride, on the other hand, exalts itself at the expense of others.
It is competitive and jealous, and often arrogant. Christ simply

reveals Himself as the one and only Saviour for the benefit of His listeners. Truth is not pride. He never advanced Himself through falsehood, nor by debasing others.

Humility then, or lowliness, is God-awareness; it is associated with "wisdom." Wisdom, knowledge of God's Word, helps a man to recognize the folly of mental attitude sin*. When we begin to restrain the sins of our thought pattern, we are free to develop the Mind of Christ, a thought pattern of grace and love. "But with the lowly is wisdom." Its emphasis is on the proper MENTAL ATTI-TUDE, which is in harmony with divine viewpoint*.

Thrust 2: Divine Norms and Standards

An antithetical distich[3] in Proverbs 11:3 illustrates the second thrust,

> *The integrity of the upright shall guide them,*
> *But the perverseness of transgressors shall destroy them.*
> *Proverbs 11:3*

Discernment or understanding is the goal of the second thrust. It comes from wisdom, as do the other two thrusts. The word "integrity" in Hebrew is *tummah* and means simplicity and completeness, an honest heart that is minus the duplicity inherent in human viewpoint*. The New Testament defines this as "single-ness of mind," (Acts 2:46), and "unworldly simplicity" as is suggested by Moulton and Milligan[4] in their word studies.

As the believer learns more and more divine viewpoint*, he develops a frame of reference* that enables him to discern between the various subtleties and facades, and make judgments between good and evil, judgments perhaps between divine good* and human good*. These will "guide" him, and will keep him within the will of God. But prior to every decision there ought to be the exercise of discernment, a weighing of the alternatives. Un-

---

[3]An antithetical distich is a two-line poem which teaches by opposite illus-trations, by contrasts of positive and negative.

[4]James Moulton and George Milligan, *Vocabulary of the Greek New Testa-ment*, Grand Rapids, Michigan: Eerdmans, 1949.

fortunately, very few decisions in life are clearly black and white to our human perception. Only the wisdom of God can equip us to correctly discern the relative worth of things, and then make our decisions and act upon them. The importance of discernment cannot be over-stressed, because every decision we make in life has some effect, either direct or subtle, on all subsequent ones. Perhaps the weight of this principle is best expressed in poetry,

> Two roads diverged in a yellow wood,
> And sorry I could not travel both
> And be one traveler, long I stood
> And looked down one as far as I could . . .
>
> Then took the other, as just as fair,
> And having perhaps the better claim,
> Because it was grassy and wanted.wear . . .
>
> Yet knowing how way leads on to way
> I doubted if I should ever come back . . .
> Two roads diverged in a wood, and I —
> I took the one less traveled by,
> And that has made all the difference.[5]

This poem illustrates graphically, via a road metaphor, the significance of decision making. The Christian, like the traveller in Mr. Frost's poem, frequently chooses the less obvious alternative, the grassier or less-travelled route,[6] since eternal values are often in opposition to immediate, human, temporal values. Most decisions are bothersome, if not impossible, to reverse; and each one "makes all the difference" to each later decision.

The second line of Proverbs 11:3 anticipates destruction for the perverse man. In Hebrew, perverseness *(seleph)* is "crookedness." The "transgressor" sins because his mind is crooked; he is on negative volition* toward Bible doctrine and he is unenlightened by the Word of God. Consequently when he must make a decision, his frame of reference is in disorder. It may be based on his particular lust pattern or perhaps it is based on human

---

[5]Robert Frost, *The Complete Poems of Robert Frost,* "The Road Not Taken," New York: Holt, Rinehart & Winston, Inc., 1967, p. 131.

[6]This is illustrated in the Sermon on the Mount, Matthew 7:13-14, concerning the wide gate and the narrow gate and their end results.

viewpoint*. Either of these will circumvent, divert, distort or erode the simple principles of God. Such are clearly in His Word, and known to the "upright." The "perverseness of the transgressors" distorts their discernment, a state originally brought about by the activity of their Old Sin Natures* and resulting in the eventual destruction of their souls.

The Hebrew word for destroy, *shadad,* means to ruin or spoil. Our decisions are exercises of free will. We bring personal ruin to our lives when we lack the wisdom necessary to make right decisions. Conversely, when we have the necessary wisdom, we have the discernment to make those right decisions that will guide us in God's Will and spell success. Thus, "wisdom is the principal thing; therefore get wisdom, and with all thy getting, get understanding." (Proverbs 4:6) It will provide DIVINE NORMS AND STANDARDS which will develop discernment and objectivity, and the knowledge of right and wrong.

Thrust 3: Overt Activity

A false balance is an abomination to the Lord,
But a just weight is his delight.
Proverbs 11:1

The emphasis in the third thrust in Proverbs is on overt behavior, and the example selected for the illustration is a business norm and standard. This is the picture of a merchant selling goods by weight. God abhors dishonesty in business, here exemplified by a dishonest pair of scales. This is another antithetical distich, and with contrast it points out conversely how delighted God is by the work of an honest businessman who, through his adherance to a divine principle, contributes to the stability of the entire society.

No matter how many hours one may spend in one kind of religious activity or another, none of it will mean much to God or man unless one *lives* according to Divine Norms and Standards. The basic quality God wants and man should expect is a uniform standard of honesty in each and every facet of one's life. A tempted housewife who keeps some extra change given her by an overworked grocery clerk may not compare with a bank robber or a jewel thief in the eyes of the law. But if she is a Christian, she may shatter her divine relationship even more than the bank robber or jewel thief who had no such relationship to begin with. Therefore, in a sense, the insult to God may be greater.

A business man with a uniformly honest set of principles will likely succeed, and perhaps his success will be great. A believer can be wealthy and successful (though still lowly) as he recognizes the source of his wealth, God, and minimizes the importance of his financial status. His wealth is obtained through hard work, intelligent planning, good merchandise and social concern rather than through such alternatives as laziness, mismanagement, cheating and exploitation.

Divine Norms and Standards create a healthy climate in society. They are not based on asceticism or self-denial. A "just weight" will not result in poverty; it will result in many fair profits. Honesty, and not the aforementioned legalism*, is the primary standard for overt behavior. Wealth is a *test* of character. The Scriptures never criticize riches; they only warn, and often, against the sins which money can easily lead to, such as materialism, or worse, pride. Proverbs helps define the overt behavior pattern which pleases God. This manner of conducting one's life cannot help but have impact on society, giving further credence to the Christian faith. Thus the third thrust of Proverbs is toward action and the Divine Norms and Standards that ought to govern our OVERT BEHAVIOR.

Conclusion

The Three Thrusts of Proverbs have been dealt with, not in their order in the Scriptures, but rather in their order of importance. In reviewing them, the reader should be able to observe how they follow sequentially. First, one must conquer *mental attitude*. This is the basic problem area. By intake of Bible doctrine, we build up a Mind of Christ, which recognizes, and repents of mental attitude sin. As these sins are cleansed from our minds, then Bible doctrine can act as a *frame of reference* for discernment. Decisions then result overtly in new and *better actions*. The constant repetition of this cycle is what keeps the

Christian in balance as he progresses in the Christian Way of
Life.

> *Wisdom is the principal thing; therefore get wisdom,*
> *And with all thy getting get understanding.*
> *... exalt her ... embrace her ...*
> *A crown of glory shall she deliver to thee.*
> *Proverbs 4:7-9*

CHAPTER II

Prologue to Proverbs

BEFORE WE CAN BEGIN to exegete (explain or interpret) the various areas of doctrine in Proverbs, it is necessary to spend some time studying the structure of this poetic portion of God's Word. This book is unique among the 66 books of the Bible in that it consists entirely of proverbs, or in the Hebrew, *mashalim*. The word *mashal* refers to a short, concise statement that rules the life. The Proverbs frequently utilize colloquialisms that were familiar to David and Solomon and their contemporaries, but are little known today. Delivered in colorful and often "folksy" language, the pithy nature of these *mashalim* (poems) makes them enjoyable to study and easy to remember.

Although Proverbs 1:1 says, "The Proverbs of Solomon the son of David, king of Israel," the proverbs are not all the work of Solomon. Some were written by his father, David. David's work is found in the following sections:

Proverbs   1:7 — 9:18
19:20 — 24:34
27:1 — 29:27

This is 501 of the 885 verses in Proverbs, or about 57%.

Solomon's own contributions, comprising the remaining 43% are as follows:

Proverbs   10:1 — 19:19
25:1 — 26:28
30:1 — 31:31

The final two chapters, 30 and 31, are said to be the wisdom of two other kings, Agur and Lemuel, respectively. Many scholars claim, and this author agrees, that Agur is merely a pseudonym for Solomon. The Jewish Talmud gives six different names for Solomon and one of them is Agur. Proverbs may be credited to Solomon both as a publisher and (in part) as an author. His major source was his father, King David.

One aspect of Proverbs that makes it unique in the canon of Scripture is that the primary audience to which it is aimed is the teen-ager. Although beneficial to any age group, the ideal time to learn something by which to rule your life is while you are in your growing years. The younger one is, the easier it is to absorb and learn; and the older one becomes, the harder it is to exchange bad mental attitudes and behaviour patterns for good ones. David, the man who began this collection of proverbs, did so with a particular young man in mind, his son Solomon.

When he was a teen-ager, Amnon, David's eldest son, became a rapist. David's second eldest son, Daniel by Abigail, apparently died as a child. His third son, Absalom, murdered Amnon and later headed a rebellion against David, in which Absalom himself was killed. Naturally David, a very busy man, was disappointed. He undoubtedly blamed himself for failing to teach Amnon and Absalom Bible doctrine. The example of a busy but good father, often somewhat remote to a child, is not enough to teach a son. A child needs to learn discipline and divine viewpoint. Although David was an admirable man of God, his son Amnon was a teen-age failure and Absalom was worse, a royal rebel. David then decided to work harder in training his next son, Solomon, whom he selected to succeed him to the throne.

He knew that if Solomon were to become a wise and effective ruler, he would have to have a maximum amount of Bible doctrine. Therefore, David began to prepare these short *mashalim* to teach Solomon so that he could learn them vividly, and instantly call upon their wisdom when it was needed. We might call this the immediate reason for the writing of the proverbs. But from David's personal burden, the Holy Spirit has given to all generations this body of discernment and good sense. It is couched in such a literary style as to instruct and inspire all ages of the need and value of ruling one's life from divine viewpoint. Modern parents still have the privilege and responsibility to teach their children wisdom and the Word of God. Proverbs is a good source of this wisdom.

One of the rarest of literary gifts is the ability to present important ideas in a clear but beautiful form. The proverbs, presented in a simple and aesthetic form, contain the genius of some of the wisest men who ever lived. Since most of the proverbs use the technique of analogy or simile, they are also easily remembered. The King James Translation of the Bible does not arrange the proverbs in poetic form. However, some other translations do, such as the Berkeley Translation, which makes a study of Proverbs increasingly interesting. Ancient Hebrew poetry, like some kinds of modern English poetry, did not depend upon rhyme for its appeal. Rather it depended upon meter. Its poetic structure makes Proverbs comparative or contrasting, colorful, brief and concise, and pleasing to read. But the most important thing is that the truth behind the poetry comes through clearly.

To study the structure of the proverbs, we are going to have to learn some technical terms. The first of these is a German word, *distich*[1] (pronounced "dish-tick"). The prefix *di-* means two, and the root of the word, *stich* means line. The word is used in references to two-line poems. Two-line distichs make up the majority of the proverbs. There are six different kinds of distichs which we shall consider individually. We shall first give a definition and then several examples so that one may become familiar with each of the six kinds.

---

[1] I wish to express my indebtedness to Rev. R. B. Thieme, Jr., the first English speaking scholar to apply this stylistic analysis to the Book of Proverbs. Rev. Thieme's tape recorded lectures, *Proverbs Series: 1966* (34 2-track tapes), are available from Publications and Tape Department, Berachah Church, 5139 West Alabama, Houston, Texas 77027.

TABLE I

KINDS OF DISTICHS

Kind of Distich	Example	Structure
1. Synonymous Distich	The liberal soul shall be made fat, And he that watereth shall be watered himself also. Proverbs 11:25	Doctrine given Doctrine repeated
2. Antithetical Distich	A sound heart is the life of the flesh, But envy the rottenness of the bones. Proverbs 14:30	Positive doctrine given Negative doctrine given
3. Synthetic Distich	He that hideth hatred has lying lips, And he that uttereth a slander is a fool. Proverbs 10:18	First doctrine on subject Second doctrine on subject
4. Integral Distich	Train up a child in the way he should go and, When he is old, he will not depart from it. Proverbs 22:6	Doctrine begun Doctrine completed
5. Parabolic Distich	As a jewel of gold in a swine's snout, So is a fair woman who is without discretion. Proverbs 11:22	Illustration from life Analogous doctrine
6. Comparative Distich	Better is a dinner of herbs where love is, Than a stalled ox and hatred therewith. Proverbs 15:17	"Better than" doctrine Comparative Fact of Life

A. The Synonymous Distich

The simplest kind of distich is the *Synonymous Distich*, a two-line poem in which each line means the same thing. The first line gives a doctrine, and the second line repeats the doctrine in different words or using a different example. This method of teaching is based upon the principle of repetition. An example is found in Proverbs 11:25,

> *The liberal soul shall be made fat,*
> *AND he that watereth shall be watered also himself.*

The "liberal soul" is the person who is generous, not selfish, in his giving and sharing of what he has. The phrase "shall be made fat" is a Hebrew idiom for wealth. Therefore, the man who gives liberally will receive blessings liberally. The man in the second line is also a wealthy man, but in a particular way that can only be appreciated by inhabitants of a semi-arid country like Palestine, where water is especially valuable. This man has water on his property, possibly a good reservoir or a productive well. "He that watereth" indicates a man who is willing to share his surplus water so that his neighbors can also irrigate crops. In return for his generosity, this man too will prosper as he finds himself surrounded by prosperity.

Conversely, if he keeps his surplus water to himself, he would soon find himself without neighbors to socialize with or trade with, or without friends to help him to protect his own property. His farm would become an isolated pocket surrounded by either nothing or poverty. While the application of this proverb changes according to the civilization and setting, the principle of life expounded therein remains unchanged. If business concerns apply this principle, the benefits are reaped by not just a few, but by many. God authorizes the practice of capitalism — private ownership and management. It can be seen here that the first line of the distich states the doctrine, and the second line repeats it in different words.

B. The Antithetical Distich

The second type of distich is the *Antithetical Distich*, which communicates Bible doctrine through means of opposite statements, an antithesis. One line gives the positive side of the doctrine and the other line gives the negative side. This type of distich usually takes the form of 'If you do x-activity you will prosper, BUT if you do y-activity you will suffer.' Whereas in the synonymous distich, the conjunction is normally "and," here in the antithetical distich it is usually "but," which indicates a statement of contrast. This also is an excellent way to learn because a person learns to compare the consequences of both courses of action and thus is less likely to choose the wrong way. An antithetical distich is found in Proverbs 14:30,

> *A sound heart is the life of the flesh,*
> *BUT envy the rottenness of the bones.*

Notice that the second line of this antithetical distich begins with the word "but." A good method to compare and categorize the proverbs is to notice the little conjunction. It will provide a valuable clue in identifying the type of proverb under study, and the mode of teaching used to make the doctrine lucid.

A "sound heart" is a term for mental stability, and a stable mentality comes from a thorough knowledge and application of Bible doctrine. This line states that a *stable mind* is essential for a healthy body. What is on your mind determines much about how you feel physically. A large percentage of physical maladies can be traced to mental instability, sins. Mentally unstable people who have fear, frustration, anxiety and worry will probably not be healthy. Similarly, people who commit mental attitude sins such as envy, hostility, implacability, jealousy, and vindictiveness, may also find themselves the victims of physical or mental disorders.

There are three basic dangers to your health. The first (1) is in what you eat or drink. Your body will suffer if you fail to feed it properly. The second danger (2) is the lack of proper exercise, both mental and physical. Just as you must exercise your muscles to keep them in tone, so you must exercise your mind with proper mental attitudes such as love, joy, peace, patience and other virtues. If the first danger may be described as what one *takes* into his stomach, the second danger may be described, by contrast, as what one *fails to take* into his lungs, that is, ample oxygen needed for healthy tissues. The third danger (and usually the greatest danger) is (3) in what you put into your mind. The second line of the proverb makes this most clear. "Envy the rottenness of the bones." Envy is a mental attitude sin, which can cause your physical system to react all over. It can put your body, mind and soul into turmoil. "Rottenness of the bones" is an idiom meaning an aching, decrepit, tumultuous, turbulent feeling. So a stable mental attitude is an important source of good health and the source of mental stability is Bible doctrine.

Proverbs 17:22 is another antithetical distich that has a meaning similar to the one just discussed regarding health.

> *A merry heart doeth good like a medicine,*
> *BUT a broken spirit drieth the bones.*

A "merry heart" is a happy mental attitude. It is happy primarily because it is occupied with divine viewpoint. One can frequently overlook a minor discomfort when he is particularly happy. A merry heart works like a medicine to counterbalance the discomforts caused by adverse overt circumstances. This is the positive side of the doctrine, but there is a negative side also. A defeated, down-hearted, miserable person has a "broken spirit." This attitude is usually the result of allowing one's mind to occupy itself with the details of life*, rather than the Lord Jesus Christ and His way of life. They leave one empty, purposeless, perhaps compromised, broken in the realm of the spirit. They leave the soul as miserable as 'dry bones', an idiom for an aching body. Whether the details of life, such as friends, health, or freedom, are good or bad, a Christian *should not depend on them* for his happiness or his mental equilibrium, his stability. "Man doth not live by bread alone (a symbol for the details of life), but by every word that proceedeth out of the mouth of God." This is what our Lord taught concerning His great temptation in the wilderness, Matthew 4:4.

If one's happiness and stability depend on details of life, one is defeated already. But if one occupies his mind with the Word of God "which liveth and abideth forever," his stability is based on something which will neither change nor end. Therefore one's mental attitude should not fluctuate with external fortunes, for they often prove unstable. People with "broken spirits" will frequently indulge in other sins such as envy or jealousy of those who have the details that he or she lacks. Jealousy and envy can never co-exist with a merry heart, so as your merry heart is defeated, so is your good health. Bible doctrine does not expect Christians to lead a miserable, ascetic or guilt-ridden existence;

rather when properly taught it points the way to a full, rich life and a glorious eternity.

There is another antithetical distich that deals with a subject germane to the whole book of Proverbs. It is found in Proverbs 15:5,

> *A fool despiseth his father's instruction,*
> *BUT he that regardeth reproof is prudent.*

Proverbs frequently uses the word "fool" to refer to a person who ignores the knowledge that he has. Under the divine institution of family life, it is the father's responsibility to teach his children doctrine. It is the children's obligation to heed that instruction. If the child does not appreciate ("despiseth") his father's teachings, he is a fool and corrupts the divine institution of family (as well as the divine institution of nationalism, as will be seen in a later chapter). This is the negative side of the doctrine, since nobody wants to be characterized as a fool. The child who pays heed to his father's verbal disciplines ("regardeth reproof") is prudent. That is, he is wise. He will succeed in life whereas the fool will create misery and find failure.

C. The Synthetic Distich

The third type of distich is called a *Synthetic Distich*. The word "synthetic," from the verb "to synthesize," means a combination of several different parts put together to form a whole. A synthetic distich gives more than one teaching or doctrine concerning one subject. Our first example is found in Proverbs 10:18,

> *He that hideth hatred has lying lips,*
> *AND he that uttereth a slander is a fool.*

This type of proverb uses "and" to link the two lines as did the synonymous distich. There, it linked two similar or parallel statements while here it joins two different statements. The central subject in this distich is "lip sinning."

If a person has hatred in his heart, a mental attitude sin, the only way he can hide it is through the overt sin of lying. This kind of lying takes the form of saying sweet things to hide or mask the hatred lying within. The proverb says this man is a fool. A fool is a person who knows the academics of doctrine but does not apply them. This man obviously knows his hatred is wrong, or he would not feel the need to lie to camouflage it. But instead of working to rid himself of the hatred, rather he works to hide it and thereby commits a second sin. This is what we call "chain-sinning." David and Bathsheba knew something about that; their initial sin of illicit lust finally let to murder, with Uriah as the ultimate victim.

The second line says that a slanderer is also a fool. Slander is a lie about another person for the purpose of destroying that person's character or reputation. This is another type of lip sin that is equally dangerous and equally foolish. Lip sinning is clearly one of the worst sins that one can participate in. In Proverbs 6:16-19, seven things are listed as "an abomination" unto the Lord. Three of the seven are lip sins: a lying tongue, a false witness and a sower of discord.

D. The Integral Distich

A fourth type of distich is the *Integral Distich*, in which the first line starts a thought and the second line completes it. An integral distich is found in Proverbs 13:14,

> *The law of the wise is a fountain of life,*
> *To depart from the snares of death.*

The "law" refers to the academics of Bible doctrine and the "wise" are those who apply that doctrine. The word "fountain" includes the concept of a source, and implies that the source of life is in the application of Bible doctrine. The second line, which completes this thought, contains a reference to death. But here the "death" is spiritual. When the believer sins and does not rebound*, he becomes spiritually dead and acts from energy of his Old Sin Nature rather than from the Holy Spirit. However, the "law of the wise" should enable the believer to recognize sin in his life and motivate him to confess it to God so that he can avoid the "snares of (spiritual) death." Thus he can continue in maximum productivity for the Lord.

Another integral distich is found in Proverbs 19:20,

> *Hear counsel, and receive instruction,*
> *That thou mayest be wise in thy latter end.*

This proverb begins in an imperative mood. It instructs the believer to seek out "counsel," or a Bible class, and "receive instruction." "Instruction" is categorical teaching on the correct means of living the Christian life. The second line begins with "that," which introduces a purpose clause. What is the purpose of going to hear a Bible teacher? "That thou mayest be wise." Wisdom is the application of knowledge, and one cannot apply what he has not learned. The phrase "in thy latter end" means as one moves through life, he can continue to apply what has been learned in former years. So the best time to learn is while one is young so that there can be a maximum number of well-spent and successful years. Hence, Proverbs is oriented to the teen-ager.

Yet another integral distich dealing with children can be found in Proverbs 22:6,

Train up a child in the way he should go,
And when he is old, he will not depart from it.

The way that children should go is according to the Plan of God. Therefore, parents want to give their children divine viewpoint so that their volition will be synonymous with the Will of God. The word "train" deserves some special attention.

The most common use of the word "train" is in the field of athletics. For an athlete, training is a discipline of daily exercise. The good athlete knows that no matter how cold and wet it looks outside at six o'clock in the morning, no matter how much he would like to get another hour of sleep, he must force himself up out of bed and outside for that morning run. If he ignores training today, it will be twice as hard tomorrow. If he ignores it tomorrow as well, he will probably forget it completely the day after. After three days of failing to train, he will never finish the race on the day of the meet.

The same principle applies in the training of a child. It not only demands daily doses of Bible doctrine, but occasionally it involves disciplining the natural desires which are contrary to the "way he should go." There are both *academics* and *discipline*.

"When he is old, he will not depart from it." There is a time lapse between the first and the second line, however. The human being does not go directly from being a "child" to being "old"; there is a period in between called adolescence, the teen-age era which is a danger period, as David realized with Amnon. Just as the body undergoes major alterations during this period, so does the mind. During this period of change, it may seem that the training has been for naught. Any parent of teen-agers will know what is meant here. Every child goes through a period of minor rebellion and thinking that he knows more than his parents. But, if he (and the parents) can survive this strain until he reaches adulthood, conditions will often smooth out again, IF HE HAS HAD THE CORRECT TRAINING AS A CHILD. This is a promise of God and need not be doubted; if the parents have fulfilled their initial obligation in rearing the child, they should be able to faith-rest through the temporary hard times of adolescence.

A good integral distich to follow that last one is Proverbs 22:15,

> *Foolishness is bound in the heart of a child,*
> *BUT the rod of correction shall drive it far from him.*

Does any child have to be taught disobedience? Does any child naturally behave correctly? The answer to both questions is emphatically, "No!" Lovable as little children are, they are natural beings with a sin nature inherited from Adam. Since in their earliest years, they are unable to categorize Bible doctrine and respond to it, they cannot be wise. So, conversely, they are foolish. After the age of 10 or 12, a parent can usually begin to reason with a child, but in his younger years, a parent must resort to physical means, "the rod of correction."[2] A wise amount of corporal punishment (discipline) is healthy because it normally leads to the results described in the proverb listed above. Conversely, it might be deduced that Satan's primary rule for rearing future "hell-raisers" is, "Don't spank a child when he misbehaves, he might think you don't love him." Parents and other family members who succumb to this line of reasoning encourage disobedience and rebellion. They pay dearly for their contributions to Operation Absalom.

The next integral distich to be observed is Proverbs 22:10,

---

[2]Author's Note. One word of important advice is needed for the disciplining parent: always use an inanimate object to spank a child, never the hand. The child too often translates his inner frustration to the object used in spanking, and if a "rod" is used the child learns to respect his parents' use of the 'weapon' without hating the hand that uses it.

Cast out the scorner, and contention shall go out;
Yea, strife and reproach shall cease.

Again one notes the imperative mood, and here again it sounds as if Proverbs is becoming a disciplinarian. The address is obviously to a group of believers rather than to the individual, and the order is to get rid of one of their members, the "scorner." This is Operation Elimination. A "scorner" is one who criticizes authority, and the authority in a group of believers is the Bible, the teacher, or the pastor. The scorner is the person who undermines the teaching of the church, and refuses to submit to the doctrine being taught. Should the entire format of the church or group be changed to please this one "scorner"? No, better the one critic remove himself, or be removed, from the congregation.

The first line then has told us what to do and the second line gives us the results of that action, "strife and reproach" will end. People have to be relaxed to learn, and how can they relax in an atmosphere of strife? Once the scorner is gone, the mood of the congregation is happier, healthier and hence more productive. This may sound like harsh doctrine, but the entire ministry for a body of believers cannot be allowed to suffer because of the strife caused by one member. Certainly someone should try to reach him first, in love, advising him to "straighten up." But if that fails and the person persists, he needs to be "cast out."

E. The Parabolic Distich

The fifth type of proverb is the parabolic distich, in which the first line gives an illustration and the second line gives the doctrine, or vice versa. This takes its name from the word *parable* which is the method of teaching so effectively used by Christ in the New Testament. Through the use of a literal example, a spiritual principle is clarified. A very colorful parabolic distich is seen in Proverbs 11:22,

As a jewel of gold in a swine's snout,
So is a fair woman who is without discretion.

The word "jewel" is actually a valuable ring in the Hebrew. You can imagine how ludicrous it would be to waste a beautiful gold ring in adorning the nose of an ugly (and unclean) swine.

So one may comprehend what a waste of natural beauty it is to have a lovely woman who has no "discretion," no understanding of right or wrong, no Bible doctrine. Such is a blend of beauty and brutishness, a bizarre and disgusting mixture.

Another parabolic distich is Proverbs 25:11. In this proverb, one finds the doctrine coming first, and the parable or example second.

> *A word fitly spoken is*
> *Like apples of gold in pictures of silver.*

The "word fitly spoken" is the right thing said at precisely the right time. It may be considered timely advice. The parable in the second line is a more esoteric Hebrew idiom. "Apples of gold in pictures of silver" is a lovely picture in a beautiful frame, sometimes a silvery, mirror-like tray. Any person who values art knows that great care must be exercised in choosing a frame for any given work. In the wrong frame, even the most masterful painting may look awkward. But, given a complementary frame, the painting and frame together achieve a harmonious aesthetic relationship. So it is with words. Even the wisest statements may sound foolish when spoken out of context, or at the improper time. But at exactly the needed moment, they achieve their maximum effect, whether it be consolation, direction or reproof.

Proverbs 27:15 contains another interesting parabolic distich about contentious people.

> *A continual dropping in a very rainy day,*
> *And a contentious woman are alike.*

If you have ever had to listen to a leak on the roof on a rainy day, you can picture this parable. The monotonous dripping begins by being merely annoying. But after some time you feel like you are being slowly and systematically driven mad. A contentious woman is just as unpleasant as that. She never gives up nagging and criticizing.

No vice can escape the chiding of the proverbs. Proverbs 26:9 deals with drunkards and fools,

> *As a thorn goeth up into the hand of a drunkard,*
> *So is a parable in the mouth of fools.*

When a man is completely intoxicated, he ceases to feel pain because the alcohol acts as an anesthetic. Consequently, if he sets his hand down on a thorn he will not feel any pain. Just as the drunkard is not aware of the thorn in his palm, neither is a fool aware of the merit and value to be gathered from the scriptures such as Proverbs. He may have enough knowledge to perhaps even quote or paraphrase many lines of scripture, but without the filling of the Holy Spirit to give him understanding, he is still a fool who cannot comprehend and apply the spiritual meaning behind the words. As Paul said, "The natural man receiveth not the things of the Spirit of God; for they are foolishness to him . . . because they are spiritually discerned." (I Corinthians 2:14)

F. The Comparative Distich

The last of the two-line proverbs is the *Comparative Distich*, which usually utilizes the conjunction "better than" to compare two things. The first example is given in Proverbs 15:17,

BETTER *is a dinner of herbs where love is,*
THAN *a stalled ox and hatred therewith.*

A dinner of herbs is clearly a poor man's meal, as is a thin watery soup perhaps flavored with no more than a few spices, or a dish of cornflakes in our time. It does not sound particularly appetizing. But if it is eaten in a loving atmosphere, it is nourishing to the body and soul alike. It is better than filet mignon eaten in an atmosphere of envy, jealousy or hatred. A "stalled ox" is a Hebrew idiom for a rich man's feast. This proverb may apply to social life. The situation may occur where you are invited to dine sumptuously with someone who only uses that opportunity to share with you the envy, jealousy or hatred he holds toward a mutual acquaintance. His misery seeks your company. This kind of menu is to be shunned, while the simpler kind of menu mentioned above may be quite beneficial, particularly when eaten in an atmosphere of appreciation for the God of Heaven and Earth and a feeling of appreciation for those with whom you dine, minus any vicious gossip about a third party. Beware of those who would invite you to a feast in order to woo your allegiance against another. It will not lead to much good, good food notwithstanding.

The last distich to be discussed, another comparative distich, is found in Proverbs 21:19. Its doctrine is something like the previous proverb.

> *It is BETTER to dwell in the wilderness,*
> *THAN with a contentious and an angry woman.*

The wilderness is a lonely location. Since most people desire some amount of social contact, the wilderness is considered to be an unpleasant place. Living there would be better, says the proverb, than living with a "contentious" and "angry" woman. It was observed earlier that a contentious person is like a dripping leak in the roof. An angry woman can be just as annoying. She has some grudge, perhaps from an external cause or perhaps from an internal cause and she does not have the inner ability to cope with the tendency. She cannot always be held to blame for the fact that she may have problems, but she is responsible for her mental attitude toward them. Anger is not a bona fide mental attitude. In her anger, she can only make life miserable for her mate and for her family as well as for herself. She cancels out more proper mental attitudes such as love, patience and peace.

We have now categorized all six types of *distichs*. But there are some other kinds of *stichs* that are occasionally found in Proverbs. These are composed of various numbers of lines. The next step beyond the two-line poem is a *tristich*, a three-line poem. There are only a few of these three-line proverbs, such as Proverbs 28:10. This kind of *stich* will not be studied here.

G. The Synonymous Tetrastich

The next step beyond the tristich is the *tetrastich*, tetra- meaning four; so this is a four-line proverb. It was noticed with the distichs that there are several different categories. So it is with the tetrastichs where there are also found several different categories. The first one to be examined is a *Synonymous Tetrastich*. An example is found in Proverbs 24:3-5.

> *Through wisdom is an house builded,*
> *And by understanding it is established;*
> *And by knowledge shall the chambers be filled*
> *With all precious and pleasant riches.*

A basic concept of the word "wisdom" is by now beginning to

take form. It is recalled that "wisdom" is a combination of knowledge and application. One is never truly wise until he *applies* what he *knows* to overt *actions*.[3] So "wisdom" is the means of building a "house," a constructive action. The term "house" here is general enough to allow application to several levels of meaning.

On the first level, one might refer to the house of the individual's soul. A well built house must be able to stand up under varying external circumstances, such as wind and rain.[4] Hence wisdom, the application of Bible doctrine, will enable one's soul-house to withstand any external circumstances that life may have in store.

As is noted in line 3, the house has more than one chamber.[5] In the soul, these chambers (rooms) include (1) the conscience chamber, (2) the intellect chamber, (3) the self-conscious chamber, (4) the volition chamber, (5) the emotion chamber and (6) the chamber of the old sin nature.* Five of the chambers, the five which do not include the old sin nature, should depend upon Bible doctrine for their operational strength. In the case of the sixth chamber, the old sin nature, we should depend upon Bible doctrine for its restraint, for "boxing it in."

Another level of meaning for "house" may be the family. The family also needs a firm foundation. It also has different chambers such as parent-child relationships, monetary values, behaviour patterns, social circles and health conditions. The Word of God has categories of doctrine that apply to all of these areas. When applied, they will yield a stable, happy family life.

The "house" may also refer to the life of a church, whose chambers might include such areas as relationships between the members, quality of officers, economic prosperity, and worship modes. Our national entity, the United States of America, could

[3]William Glasser, M.D., suggests the importance of responsibility for one's actions based upon known behavior norms as an aid to establish proper mental attitudes. This concept of psychiatric therapy coincides with the concept we outline in the function of the soul in this book in Chapter IX. William Glasser, *Reality Therapy — A New Approach to Psychiatry*, New York: Harper and Row, 1965.

[4]This analogy, perhaps based on this very proverb, is found in the last section of the Sermon on the Mount by our Lord, Matthew 7:24-28. This is indicative that the Book of Proverbs is a major background for the Sermon on the Mount, which more or less codifies the ethics for the Christian Way of Life.

[5]See Figures 7 and 8, page 150.

also be called a "house" whose chambers would include economic conditions, form of government, health standards, moral standards, and quality of education. In other words, any entity, or "house," which is constructed with "wisdom," or Bible doctrine, will be well built.

The word "understanding" in line 2 is the ability to discern right from wrong. The thing that teaches one to discern right from wrong is Bible doctrine. Understanding will "establish" your house or stabilize it.

The second half of the tetrastich speaks of "knowledge," which is a reference to the academic categories of doctrine. Just as there are different chambers of the house to be filled, so there are different shelves in each chamber. The Mentality serves as the main library of the soul. Each shelf is designed to carry a different category of doctrine.

Just as we categorized the different types of distichs, so we can categorize the many different areas of doctrine. There is a shelf for Christian Life Techniques, a shelf for dispensations, and a shelf for prophecy. When many of these shelves are filled in the chamber of the soul called Mentality, one has a magnificent collection of "precious" and "pleasant" riches.

H.   The Synthetic Tetrastich

A *Synthetic Tetrastich*, like a synthetic distich, gathers several doctrines around a single subject. A synthetic tetrastich whose central subject is the Word of God is found in Proverbs 30:5-6,

> *Every word of God is pure;*
> *He is a shield unto those who put their trust in him.*
> *Add thou not unto his words,*
> *Lest he reprove thee, and thou be found a liar.*

Since "every word of God is pure," all doctrine is equally important and every word is absolute truth. The third line warns us not to alter God's holy word, because its own inner consistency will rise up and prove us mistaken. One example is the theories of the cynical "higher critics" from the school of German rationalism. Their criticisms are repeatedly silenced by new findings such as archaeological discoveries which continue to validate the scriptures' literalness.

I. The Integral Tetrastich

There is an *Integral Tetrastich* found in Proverbs 30:17,

The eye that mocketh at his father,
And despiseth to obey his mother,
The ravens of the valley shall pick it out,
And the young eagles shall eat it.

This proverb warns in strong terms that any son or daughter who ignores the teaching and authority of his parents will have to pay the price. They will be the victims of their own revolution and will suffer at the hands of those whom God has ordained as His "ministers of righteousness" to maintain law and order. (Romans 13:1-5) Political rebellion is almost always preceded by rebellion against parents.

J. The Integral Pentastich

The five-line proverbs take their name from the prefix *penta-*, meaning five. A *Pentastich* is a five-line poem in which each succeeding line further completes or fulfills the thought. Such a proverb is found in Proverbs 23:6-7,

Eat thou not the bread of him who hath an evil eye,
Neither desire thou his dainty meats,
For as he thinketh in his heart, so is he.
Eat and drink, saith he to thee;
But his heart is not with thee.

The first two lines here give the doctrine, and the last three lines give reasons for the doctrine. Again one finds an imperative that pertains to our social life. The "eye" is called the window of the soul, and it can reveal the mental attitude within. Many times one can discern a man's thoughts just by looking in his eyes. If an "evil eye" is discerned, you are to avoid dining with him and thus you avoid letting his tempting fare subvert your mental attitude. "Neither desire thou his dainty meats."

He is very likely only offering you a good meal so that he can open you to his suggestions; you will then listen to his evil talk.

Perhaps he wants to extract some information or to slander someone else, or possibly to express feelings of jealousy or hatred,
and he wants you to share those feelings.

As line 3 warns us, whatever is in his heart defines him. If he
is thinking sin, he is sinful. He is not really concerned about you,
even though he may be playing the role of a thoughtful and
generous host. The primary thing on his mind is his own sin,
the multiplication of his own sin, and the drawing you in to
·share it. If you go on to read Proverbs 23:8, you will note that
if you stay around long enough, you will "lose thy sweet words."
In other words, you will begin to share his mental attitude sin.
You cannot afford to risk this danger. This is not an invitation to
judge and hate other people for their failures. It is simply a
warning to be on the alert for them and avoid them. It is discretion;
it is discrimination. It is better to love such people from afar.

K. A Hexastich

There is also a six-line proverb called a *Hexastich*. We can find
one in Proverbs 23:12-14,

> *Apply thine heart unto instruction,*
> *And thine ears to the words of knowledge.*
> *Withhold not correction from the child;*
> *For if thou beatest him with the rod, he shall not die,*
> *Thou shalt beat him with the rod,*
> *And shalt deliver his soul from hell.*

To "apply thine heart" is to exercise volition or motivation with
regard to the study and observance of Bible doctrine. This is not
the sort of thing that comes easily, for it is against the inclination
of the old sin nature. Therefore, self-discipline must be used.
The second line informs us that the "ears" must also be used.
You must listen for the details of Bible doctrine, here called
"knowledge." This too takes discipline. It is easy to sit through a
Bible class or a sermon and, if the lesson presentation happens
to be rather dry, to look as if you are absorbing the lesson when
in actuality your mind is concentrating on the way the teacher
parts his hair, the design of his tie, or the planning of your Sunday
afternoon. Such a listener retains little if anything. A person who
is eager for knowledge will discipline himself to listen for content,

not for an exciting technique of speaking or teaching. Many people sit through sermons and remember only the jokes. A true scholar concentrates on the message, not the messenger.

The last four lines of the hexastich illustrate the reason for applying one's heart (or mind) to doctrine. The example is a child. The child, as was learned earlier, must occasionally be forced into the correct behavior pattern when he is too young to be persuaded through the means of verbal logic. Many parents are afraid, or perhaps too lazy, to use this means of discipline, even though the Word of God encourages it. "He shall not die," says David. He may sound like it. But this is usually an act to work on a parent's sympathy and deter further punishment. The important thing to learn is that, if you discipline the child, you may cause him some temporary discomfort, but you save him from eternal anguish in hell.

L. The Octostich

The last "stich" we deal with is the *Octostich*, an eight-line proverb. One of these is Proverbs 6:16-19,

> *These six things doth the Lord hate;*
> *Yea, seven are an abomination unto him;*
> *A proud look, a lying tongue,*
> *And hands that shed innocent blood,*
> *An heart that deviseth wicked imaginations,*
> *Feet that are swift in running to mischief,*
> *A false witness that speaketh lies,*
> *And he that soweth discord among brethren.*

God abhores seven things and He is very specific about what they are. "A proud look" is a Hebrew idiom for a man who has such a mental attitude of pride that it shows through his countenance. "A lying tongue" is an idiom for people who are compulsive liars. Sometimes they even tell lies that have no ulterior motive. Line 4 describes murder (which is the only overt sin in the group). "A wicked imagination" is an uncontrolled mentality that is always dreaming of evil things to do to people for its own pleasure. This might be the man who has lust in his heart when he looks at attractive ladies, or envy and revenge in his heart when he sees a person more prosperous or successful than he. Those swift feet in line 6 belong to the local busy-bodies. They are the people who have to spread every rumor they hear, no matter how ill-founded. "A false witness" tells lies about other people, usually in order to damage or deceive. The person "that soweth discord" is that person who gave those dinner parties that we read of earlier. He likes to create disharmony in a society, perhaps in a church, perhaps in a faculty, perhaps in an athletic team or in a nation. Of these seven, six are mental attitude sins.

At this point, our technical introduction to the Book of Proverbs is completed. The prime purpose in this chapter has been to familiarize the reader with the literary structure of the book. In so doing we have dealt with a variety of colorful proverbs. It is hoped that each reader will now be able to read into Proverbs an added dimension, a dimension which will add enjoyment as well as comprehension as each person categorizes for himself the various kinds of *stichs*.

The remainder of the chapters of this book will deal with specific areas of doctrine found in the Book of Proverbs. Even though the group of proverbs that we have seen in this introduction has not been consistent in subject matter, two important themes emerge already. The first is the emphasis on getting Bible doctrine into the mentality, storing knowledge of divine viewpoint in the soul. This theme will be seen again and again throughout the book.

The second great theme we have seen is the urging to avoid mental attitude sin. People are often satisfied with themselves because they avoid such overt sins as theft, murder or adultery. In their self-admiration, and superficial righteousness, they fail to pay heed to the less overt, or less violent sins such as envy, grudge-holding, hatred, jealousy and pride. These sins, though internal, are just as evil to the eyes of a perfectly righteous God as are the more overt sins just mentioned.

In a sense these covert or mental-attitude sins might be viewed as worse. They may be committed by a Christian, indwelled by the Holy Spirit, who has no excuse for failing to live up to divine norms and standards. These sins are just as destructive to the Christian's output of divine good as are more overt sins. The point is that none of us can afford to commit mental attitude sins. It will allow evil to prevail; it will reflect no glory to God; it will hurt others; it will destroy our own happiness, our own health, our prosperity and our potential to achieve God's destiny for each particular life. Mental attitude sins, Bible doctrine and divine viewpoint are widely discussed in the proverbs.

CHAPTER III

The Wages of Wisdom

My son, forget not my law;
But let thine heart keep my commandments:
For length of days, and long life, and peace shall they add
*   to thee.*
Let not mercy and truth forsake thee:
Bind them about thy neck;
Write them upon the table of thine heart;
So shalt thou find favor and good understanding in the
*   sight of God and man.*

Trust in the Lord with all thine heart;
And lean not unto thine own understanding.
In all thy ways acknowledge him,
And he shall direct thy paths.
Be not wise in thine own eyes;
Fear the Lord and depart from evil.
It shall be health to thy navel, and marrow to thy bones.

Honor the Lord with thy substance,
And with the firstfruits of all thine increase:
So shall thy barns be filled with plenty,
And thy presses shall burst out with new wine.

My son, despise not the chastening of the Lord;
Neither be weary of his correction:
For whom the Lord loveth he correcteth;
Even as a father the son in whom he delighteth.

Happy is the man that findeth wisdom,
And the man that getteth understanding.
For the merchandise of it is better than the merchandise
*   of silver,*
And the gain thereof than fine gold.
She is more precious than rubies;
And all the things thou canst desire are not to be
*   compared unto her.*
Length of days is in her right hand,
And in her left hand riches and honor.
Her ways are ways of pleasantness, and all her paths are
*   peace.*
She is a tree of life to them that lay hold upon her:
And happy is every one that retaineth her.
Proverbs 3:1-20

The section of Proverbs that is under consideration in this chapter covers a gamut of doctrines. The chosen title is "The Wages of Wisdom" since the common theme is the benefits which come from heeding Bible doctrine. The third and fourth chapters of Proverbs illustrate a beautiful principle. Chapter Three is David's advice to Solomon, and apparently Solomon paid attention, because Chapter Four is Solomon's advice to his son, Rehoboam.

Unfortunately, Rehoboam did not listen to his father, so the heritage of wisdom ended with the young prince. But at least there were three generations of Bible teaching being passed on from father to son. David's success as a king was perpetuated by Solomon, because Solomon learned the wisdom of his father. Rehoboam, in contrast, started Israel down the path to destruction. It takes only four "minus doctrine generations" to totally destroy a nation.[1] What parents communicate to their children determines what the next generation will do with their society, their nation, and the world.

[1]This will be demonstrated in Chapter V, Part 2, Agur's Quaternaries

The "Payoff" of Bible Doctrine

My son, forget not my law,
But let thine heart keep my commandments:
For length of days, and long life,
And peace shall they add to thee.
Let not mercy and truth forsake thee;
Bind them upon thy neck;
Write them upon the table of thine heart;
So shalt thou find favor and good understanding in the
   sight of God and man.
Proverbs 3:1-4

The need to remember the law of God' is widely recognized, but how is that achieved? There are basically three ways to teach a child to remember the law of God:

1. By a system of Categories
2. By Repetition
3. By Example

The laws or principles are best taught meticulously and carefully, hence categorically, rather than just presented in a haphazard manner with the hope that the child will retain some kernel of content. If a school teacher just gave children facts without categorizing them under various subject headings such as arithmetic, geography or history, the students would have a difficult time remembering the facts, much less understanding them. The same is true of doctrine. Categorization makes it easier to remember, and hence easier to apply.

The law of God must be repeated over and over; parents must not fear 'drumming it in'. Perhaps even more importantly, it must be shown through example. Most children, through the natural love and respect that they have for their parents, will imitate their parents' behavior. This is seen, for example, in the vocabulary of small boys. If you meet a small boy who swears like a veteran trooper, you can usually assume that he is only trying to sound like his Daddy, with no true sense of what he is saying. The reverse is also true. If a father exhibits kindness, consideration and patience, his children will first choose these attributes through a natural desire to imitate, and later, through the process of habit formation, those traits will become a natural part of their behavior pattern.

Now that it has been shown HOW to remember the law of the father, a more important consideration might be WHY it should be remembered. The purpose of teaching doctrine is to prepare what we call the "ready room" in the mind of the believer. If he has a "ready room" he will not have to run to a parent, pastor or teacher every time he faces a test. He can refer to his own residual knowledge and become self-sufficient and stable. More than just *memory* is involved in the mind however.

In the second line, David says, "Let thine *heart* keep my commandments." The "heart," discussed in Chapter IX, "The Essence of the Soul," is a reference to that part of the mentality that shapes the attitude. To keep a principle in the "heart" is to hold the value dear, to cherish it, to practice it because its merit is recognized. The benefits, or as we have called them, the "wages" of this attitude are eminently practical as is seen in verse 2. The first wages are in the area of *physical health;* one will gain "length of days."

Doctrine should yield a relaxed mental attitude, and a relaxed mental attitude helps to avoid psychosomatic illnesses. The next of the benefits, or "wages," of wisdom is in the area of *mental health.* Wisdom will lead to habits that take good care of both body and mind, and this will lengthen one's life.

At first glance, it may seem that a "long life" is merely a repetition of "length of days," but in the Hebrew meaning, it connotes something closer to "a full life." The relaxed mental attitude which Bible doctrine produces will enable one to study better, learn more, produce more, earn more, and enjoy all of life to the fullest. It will result in "success," which is something more than merely a "long" life. The third result, the third "wage," of wisdom is peace, which again is a mental attitude. There is much talk about "peace" today in the media. But it always refers to an external condition rather than an internal attitude. Christ spoke of peace, but with inward connotations.

> *Peace I leave with you, my peace I give unto you; not as*
> *the world giveth, give I unto you. Let not your heart be*
> *troubled, neither let it be afraid.*
> *John 14:27*

There are at least three important points to notice in our Lord's teaching. First, peace is a characteristic of divinity; *"my* peace" Christ says, indicating that it is something which transcends our earthly character. Peace then is a part of the Edification Complex*, the believer's soul reflecting the character of Christ.

Secondly, Christ emphasizes the first point by a reminder. His reminder is that His peace is something quite different than the world's concept of peace. The media tends to see peace merely as a lack of conflict, (no bombs were dropped today over the Suez as peace reigned). Rather than being a lack of overt conflict, peace is a *positive presence in the soul*, an inner harmony existing between man and his God.

Thirdly, Christ leaves no question as to His meaning of peace. It is the absence of inner turmoil; it is the absence of fear. Hence it includes calmness and courage, dynamic mental attitudes which are further "wages" of wisdom. Yet these "wages" are not the entire dividend.

Another pair of wisdom's "payoffs" is shown in verse 3, "mercy" and "truth." Mercy indicates an attitude of grace toward people, what we call *Grace Orientation* in the Edification Complex*. Truth of course is honesty, purity, sincerity. Mercy and truth are the embodiment of the ministry of Christ. "The law was given by Moses, but GRACE and TRUTH came by Jesus Christ." (John 1:17) Jesus Christ lived Bible doctrine at all times; therefore He had mercy and truth with Him always. He learned it, in His humanity, from living under the teaching of His parents. As godly parents, they taught Him divine viewpoint.

The order to "bind them (mercy and truth) about thy neck" is analogous to the use of a signet ring. In David's time, there was no such thing as a checkbook, but there was credit. The way that a person made a purchase without cash was with the imprint of his signet ring, which was carried on a chain about the neck. The print of a signet ring was a claim on the credit of the buyer.

Analogously then, the way in which you purchase respect from people is by the possession of mercy and truth which serve as a signet ring to establish your moral and spiritual credit. If you treat people with grace and honesty, they will believe what you say. This is especially important to remember in the area of witnessing. If a man is harshly critical of his companions for some minor habit which he considers a vice, and then tries to present

Christ as a loving and merciful saviour, he is not likely to make many converts. Similarly, a housewife who always borrows from her neighbors but never returns is not going to make much progress if she tries to tell them about Christ. Our mission is not to judge sinners; God is quite capable of handling that. Our obligation is to *always* treat people with maximum grace and scrupulous honesty.

The last line of verse 3 is "write them upon the table of thine heart." It advises us to have a positive heart attitude toward the value of these two previously mentioned virtues. We are to cherish mercy and truth in our "hearts," the lower chamber of our mentality. Whatever is close to our hearts, we are not likely to forget.

"So shalt thou find favor and good understanding in the sight of God and man." Verse 4 describes the impact of doctrine in society. It provides blessing for the applier in his relationships to both God and man. "So" introduces a result clause, and it might be read, 'If you fulfill the conditions of verse 3, the result will be', "favor and good understanding in the sight of God and man." While "so" usually means cause and effect in our English usage, in this case it is a *conditional* conjunction in its Hebrew usage. Again we find the perfect example in the life of Christ, of whom it was said, "Jesus increased in wisdom and stature, and in favor with God and man." (Luke 2:52)

"Thou shalt find" is the Hebrew word *matsah* which means that one arrives at a desired destination. This suggests that we are to seek the ability to have a perfect relationship with God and man. "Favor" of men is their appreciation, and "good understanding" is respect. Men may not always want to be around you, because your good example may activate their guilt complexes. However, you will have appreciation and respect from them as you live doctrine. They will appreciate you partly because you do not judge and criticize them. They will also respect your honesty, and your relaxed mental attitude which will enable you to have a sense of humor.

These then are some of the "wages" of wisdom, the benefits of Bible doctrine. They include an increased length of days, a long and full life, inner peace, mercy, truth, grace, appreciation, and respect. This, then, may be called "the divine payoff," but mention has not yet been made of eternal life. Hence this is merely the pay-off in Phase II*.

The Essence of God

Many Christians worry constantly about how they can know the will of God. They keep expecting that it will be revealed to them in some dramatic, mysterious way, so they never reach the point of relaxation and trust which Proverbs reveals as the true path to Divine Guidance.

In a later chapter, a formula for the production of Divine Good is given, BD (Bible Doctrine) + FS (Filling of the Spirit) = DG (Divine Good), the "dynamic equation." In a similar manner, the means for Divine Guidance can be given, BD + F/RT = DG, or "Bible Doctrine plus the Faith-Rest Technique equals Divine Guidance." God supplies the answers, and we supply the faith that appropriates those answers.

Trust in the Lord with all thine heart;
And lean not unto thine own understanding.
In all thy ways acknowledge him
And he shall direct thy paths.
Proverbs 3:5-6

The word "trust" in Hebrew is *batach*, a wrestling term best translated as 'body slam'. Trust then is the act of body slamming our problems on God, dumping them right in His lap, "Casting all your care upon him, for he careth for you." (I Peter 5:7) We envision a Divine Hopper which is large enough to hold all the problems one can ever come up with; as the psalmist says, "Cast thy burden upon the Lord and He shall sustain thee." (Psalm 55:22)

One of the basic doctrines that is necessary to enable one to *batach* his problems is a knowledge of the *Essence of God*. The more that is known about God's character, the more one will realize that He can handle all our problems. A method of depicting God's essence is seen in Figure 1, which is called the Essence Box. It describes the character of our Creator.

We must begin with one basic assumption, the authority of the Holy Bible. Once this initial assumption has been made, the

VERACITY

(Absolute truth)
Num. 23:19;
Deut. 32:4;
John 1:14; 14:6

SOVEREIGNTY

(Absolute volition - will)
Ps. 92:8
I Tim. 6:15

IMMUTABILITY

(Unchangeability)
Ps. 33:11; Mal. 3:6;
Heb. 6:17, 18; 13:8

HOLINESS

(Righteousness
plus Justice)
Ps. 22:3) Is. 6:3;
Lk. 12:47; Rom. 7:12;
Gal. 6:7; Jas. 1:13

ETERNAL LIFE

(Ever-existing)
Deut. 32:40; Is. 41:4;
48:12;
Rom. 1:20; Rev. 1:8

OMNISCIENCE

(All knowing)
Ps. 139; Prov. 15:3;
Rom. 1:20

OMNIPRESENCE

(Existing everywhere)
Ps. 15:13; Act. 17:27

OMNIPOTENCE

(All powerful)
Job 5:8, 9; John 17:2

LOVE

(Absolute positive
affection)
John 3:16, 17;
I John 4:7-9

Divine Essence _____ Figure **1**

character of God is easily deduced through careful study of His Word. Moses, in the Pentateuch, first tells us that God is absolute Veracity, or Truth. We know then that whatever God says about Himself is true, and whatever He promises He will fulfill. One of the first things we learn in Genesis is that God is the Creator of our world. Hence we can assume that what He created He is master over, as He proved in His dealings with Adam. Therefore we can call Him the ultimate authority of the Universe, king of kings, and lord of lords. We sum up this power in the word Sovereign; whatever qualities God possesses, He possesses infinitely and absolutely. These two qualities, veracity and sovereignty, are the foundation for the Essence Box. Now we can begin to study the other, more specific characteristics of God, keeping in mind that each is infinite in nature.

1.

God is IMMUTABLE, He cannot nor will not ever change. He will never become less powerful or less loving. The "God is dead" philosophy is only one of the many heresies which is negated by this fundamental fact about God's character. If He can not change, then surely He cannot die. This quality also enhances the fact of God's veracity. Not only can He never lie, but also He will never change His mind about what He has already declared in His Word. When He says something, we can know that it is not only absolute truth, but also unchanging truth.

2.

God is HOLINESS; a combination of absolute righteousness and absolute justice. It is from this quality that we can understand our need for reconciliation to God, since we are obviously considerably less than righteous. Since God is absolute justice as well as absolute righteousness, He cannot have relationship with man without some form of propitiation (satisfaction of His holiness). Christ in His love supplied propitiation at the cross. God's wrath against the sinner was totally pacified. If a man accepts the work of Christ he moves into the position of having been reconciled to God. If a man rejects the work of Christ he must face the wrath of God's spurned love offered at Calvary.

3.

God also tells us that He is ETERNAL. This means that He

has always existed in eternity past, and He will always exist in eternity future. Any suggestion of the decreasing relevancy of God is petty in light of His eternal character.

4. 5. 6.

He is also OMNISCIENT, meaning that He knows everything. Adam found this out when he tried to hide his sin from God in the Garden of Eden. He is OMNIPRESENT, present everywhere all of the time. He is OMNIPOTENT, all powerful. There is nothing which He cannot accomplish. These last three powers should make us very secure; God *knows* all of our problems; He is *present* at every point in our lives; and He has the *power* to do anything He desires with our lives.

7.

These qualities, combined with the last characteristic of His essence, absolute LOVE, convinces us that we can indeed *batach* any of our problems on Him. He not only knows what we need; He is sympathetic and loving toward those needs. One qualification should be repeated however. Since God is holy, He is unable to express His infinite Love toward man until a certain reconciliation has taken place. This is accomplished at the point of salvation at which time Christ bears all of the blame for our sins. If we are not a part of the Body of Christ, God can only relate to us through His justice, but if we accept the sacrifice of Christ, then God is free to relate to us in love; His wrath is changed to mercy. We describe this position as being "past the point of propitiation," or on the right side of the cross, as is described in Figure 2.

The Faith-Rest Technique

If one can always keep his mind occupied with the character of God, one should be able to trust Him completely no matter what the circumstances. We can go to His promises, of which there are over 7,000 in the Bible, and know that they are all true, unchangeable, and eternal. If we know the Character of God, then it is actually blasphemous to worry, be fearful or frustrated. We have *faith* in God's character; so we rest unafraid of any circumstances that we may meet in life.

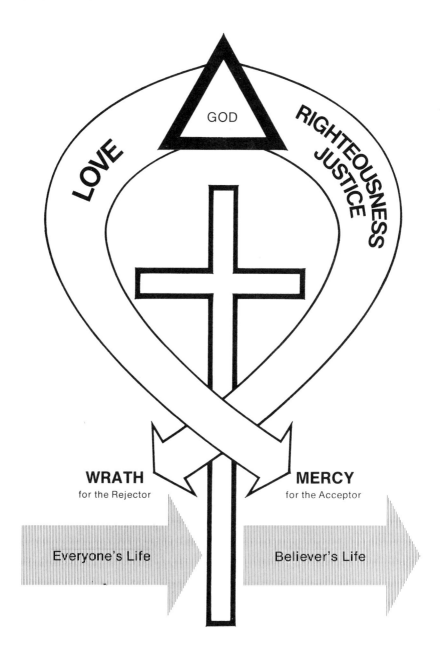

Point of Propitiation _____ Figure **2**

We have seen that Faith-Rest is the first step to Divine Guidance, "Trust in the Lord." But this same verse, Proverbs 3:5, also includes the reverse side of the same coin, "and lean not unto thine own understanding." Your own understanding is Human Viewpoint* and can never measure up to Divine Viewpoint which, as has just been learned, is omniscient. God always knows what is better for us than we ourselves. So it would be foolish to try to outguess Him in planning our lives. Human viewpoint only equals confusion and subjectivity. Verse 6 says, "In all thy ways acknowledge him." With the doctrine of the Essence Box in mind, surely you can acknowledge God to be capable of guiding your life, much more capably than you. The result of your trust will be that God will "direct thy paths." You are not going to start hearing voices from heaven saying, "Do this . . . don't do that, go here, don't go there." If you trust God, He will open the paths that He wants you to travel, He will open circles that He wants you to move toward, and close those that He disapproves or disdains.

For instance, the prospect of marriage is one about which many young people worry. A young lady may meet an eligible bachelor whom she thinks is just right for her, so she prays fervently (or desperately), "O God, let him love me, let him ask me to marry him." But this is not Faith-Rest. If she was really trusting in God, her prayer would be the same, whether an eligible bachelor was in sight or not. "Dear God, I want to get married, but I want it to be to the right man. Therefore, lead me to the one whom You know to be right for me, and direct our paths toward each other and no one else. Thy will be done." Divine Guidance then does not point out the right path in some mysterious way, but it simply makes the right path and upright path the most logical.

Divine Orientation

The next two verses point out how doctrine protects from mental attitude sins,

> *Be not wise in thine own eyes;*
> *Fear the Lord, and depart from evil.*
> *It shall be health to thy navel,*
> *And marrow to thy bones.*
> *Proverbs 3:7-8*

The greatest single enemy of the Christian life is pride, and we oppose it and protect ourselves from it by fear of the Lord. You should remember that "fear" is awe, and certainly the doctrine of God's essence should put us in awe of Him. Bible doctrine then keeps us from thinking ourselves too wise, because it makes us aware that we are nothing and God is everything. True humility is not slumped shoulders and downcast eyes. It is simply an awareness of *the source* of whatever abilities one may have received and developed. We can say with Paul, "I can do all things through Christ who strengtheneth me." (Philippians 4:13) All Christians are given spiritual gifts (or specialized abilities), but they are not a thing to be proud about, because they are not earned but are freely given. (I Corinthians 4:7)

Just as the "fear of the Lord is the beginning of wisdom," (Proverbs 1:7), so the lack of that fear, (i.e., pride or self-centeredness) is the beginning of folly. This fear of God enables us to avoid "evil." In Hebrew, this is actually "the evil," so it is a reference to that everpresent evil, the old sin nature*, which each of us possesses within. When we are occupied with Christ, we are not occupied with ourselves. It is occupation with self that is the beginning of most mental attitude sins.

Verse 8 teaches us that the result of following Bible doctrine is *mental health*, described in verse 7, which leads to *physical health*. To a person of the 10th Century B.C. a healthy "navel" was a sign of general good health, and "marrow" in the bones was a reference to physical strength. The Amplified version translates this verse as follows:

> *It shall be health to your nerves and sinews, and marrow*
> *and moistening to your bones.*
> *Proverbs 3:8*

One can never enjoy a truly healthy state if he has mental attitude sins like hatred, envy or vengeance. These can cause anything from a simple headache to an ulcer. It can cause an increase in blood pressure and a nervous breakdown. It may be called "S.I.M.," or *self-induced miseries*. Life is too short to hate; you cannot afford it. Again you apply the Faith-Rest Technique. Whatever the source of your mental irritation, God can (and in due time will) take care of it.

The Doctrine of Giving

Honor the Lord with thy substance,
And with the first fruits of thine increase;
So shall thy barns be filled with plenty,
And thy presses shall burst out with new wine.
Proverbs 3:9-10

The word "honor" here actually means to glorify; and your "substance" is everything you have. All of your substance belongs to God, not just some certain percentage of your finances. This means that you glorify God not only with the particular percentage of income that you decide to give to His work, but also by the manner in which you manage the remainder that you keep for your own use or for the needs of others. You hardly glorify God with a mismanaged budget, or by throwing money around carelessly.

Then we read about the "first fruits of thine increase," the kind of productivity that one might realize in a raise in salary, commission, or sales. The first thing we should consider is, "Now I can give more to the Lord," and not, "Now I can afford a new car." Buying new objects for personal enjoyment is not wrong in itself, the point is that we should think of God first when prosperity comes. The important part of giving is always your own mental attitude; it is not the amount, large or small. You do not glorify God if you give grudgingly; it might be just as well not to give at all, because God values the gifts of a "cheerful giver." (II Corinthians 9:7) It is *how* and *why* you give, and not *what* you give, that constitutes honoring God in your heart. Remember how much more Christ was pleased with the widow's "two mites" than with all the gold of the rich men.

Verse 10 describes the blessings of material prosperity that come to the person who glorifies God with his substance and his increase. You cannot out-give God; He blesses the willing giver. This hardly means that if you give 10% of your income, God will arrange for you to win the Irish Sweepstakes. However, if you truly honor God by managing your money wisely, you may well bring prosperity on yourself. You will not only give generously and reap generously; you will also learn to save part of your money rather than spend it all. You will learn to make sensible and constructive investments that will benefit society as well as bring prosperity to you.

Bible doctrine does not teach an arbitrary system of behavior to earn God's blessings; God does not intervene supernaturally if you follow the arbitrary procedures. Divine recompense comes because God's way is practical and will bring blessings to the believer through natural means. True Bible Christianity is a very practical way of life; you will not find a better "boss" or better wages, no matter how far you search.

The Doctrine of Discipline

My son, despise not the chastening of the Lord,
Neither be weary of his correction;
For whom the Lord loveth, he correcteth,
Even as a father the son in whom he delighteth.
Proverbs 3:11-12

God, like a father, may have to occasionally discipline us, but He always does so with grace, and it will be to our benefit if we respond according to divine viewpoint. When we are disciplined, it should result in occupation with grace; otherwise we will be occupied with ourselves and hence will gripe, complain and malign God. If we sense that we are under divine discipline, then we must first remind ourselves that God is doing it for a purpose. Then we can search our hearts to determine what it is in our lives that God is displeased with. When we discover the sin and Rebound* (I John 1:9), then the discipline turns into a blessing. We benefit because we have ridded ourselves of some area of sin. Since God loves us, He only disciplines so that we will respond positively and change our behavior pattern. It is always wise to heed the discipline of a father, especially if He is omniscient and loving as is our Heavenly Father.

Additional Benefits of Wisdom

Happy is the man that findeth wisdom,
And the man that getteth understanding;

*For the merchandise of it is better than the merchandise
      of silver,
And the gain thereof than fine gold.
She is more precious than rubies;
And all the things thou canst desire are not to be
      compared unto her.*

*Length of days is in her right hand,
And in her left hand riches and honor.
Her ways are ways of pleasantness,
And her paths are peace.
She is a tree of life to those who lay hold upon her,
And happy is every one that retaineth her.
Proverbs 3:13-18*

In the verses above, there is a reiteration of some of the benefits of wisdom. "Happy" in verse 13 is, in Hebrew, a plural word, *ashere*. Wisdom gives us two happinesses; one is overt and one is inner happiness. Only God can give you this perfect happiness, and the means of achieving it is "wisdom" and "understanding."

In verse 14 we find that wisdom, and the double happiness that it brings, is more valuable than "merchandise" (i.e., material prosperity or bank accounts). Wisdom is considerably greater than one of the most highly regarded of the details in life, Money. People who fail to recognize the merit and worth of Bible doctrine, may drive many miles to go to a lucrative job or to attend some valued recreation, but they grudgingly, if at all, yield thirty minutes of travel time to attend a Bible class. This is an inversion of values, Bible doctrine being "the chief thing" as compared to any other details.

In verses 15 through 18, David is using a special technique to reach his young teen-age son. He is depicting wisdom as a woman. Wisdom is not only more important than all the details of life; it is the means of obtaining those details. Notice that wisdom is depicted as a woman who possesses many of the most desirable details: long life, wealth, honor, pleasantness, peace, happiness. We do best to seek wisdom first, before we become overly concerned about the other accoutrements of a full life.

David ends this section by an example of true wisdom, the work of God in Creation as an illustration of supreme intelligence.

The Lord by wisdom hath founded the earth;
By understanding hath he established the heavens.
By his knowledge the depths are broken up,
And the clouds drop down the dew.
Proverbs 3:19-20

This is a beautiful way to teach doctrine, by the means of an illustration. David in effect says, "Do you want to see what wisdom can accomplish? For an example of ultimate wisdom just look at the work of God in creating the universe." These verses show the creative and sustaining power of God as evidenced by our remarkable earth environment. David mentions the rain cycle; it must have taken an enormous intellect to create such a marvel. When we see what wisdom has enabled God to accomplish, we can vaguely see what wisdom can do for us, though of course on a lesser level. God provided rain for all mankind. In the agricultural society of Israel, rain was a symbol of prosperity. Just as God's wisdom has provided a means of prosperity for the whole world, our own wisdom can provide the same for us.

Conclusion

Any secular job that we hold usually gives several different benefits, all of which may be included in the word "wages." Wisdom too pays many different kinds of benefits, none of which you will gain from a secular occupation. In conclusion, let us recapitulate those wages:

1. Length of days, verses 2, 16
2. Peace, verses 2, 17
3. Favor, good understanding, verse 4
4. Divine guidance, verse 6
5. Physical health, verse 8
6. Happiness, verses 13, 17, 18
7. Material prosperity, verses 10, 18

You can be a millionaire, and yet lack peace, health, or happiness. You can live a long life, but never achieve God's plan for your brief time on this earth. If you neglect the principle of Divine guidance, you may think you are living a highly "religious" life, yet wonder why you fail to find favor or respect from your fellow man. Whatever your shortcomings, *wisdom* can supply the answer.

She is truly a generous employer, and all that she requires is
diligence and faith. God has promised us that He is "good unto
those who wait for him, to the soul that seeketh him," (Lamenta-
tions 3:25). If we put first in our minds the "kingdom of God,"
then "all these things (details of life) shall be added unto you."
(Luke 12:31)

CHAPTER IV

The Enticement of the Wrong Crowd

To know wisdom and instruction;
To perceive the words of understanding;
To receive the instruction of wisdom,
Justice and Judgment and Equity.
To give subtilty to the simple,
To the young man knowledge and discretion.

A wise man will hear, and will increase learning;
And a man of understanding shall attain unto wise
counsels,
To understand a proverb and the interpretation,
The words of the wise and their dark sayings.

The fear of the Lord is the beginning of knowledge,
But fools despise wisdom and instruction.
My son, hear the instructions of thy father,
And forsake not the law of thy mother;
For they shall be an ornament of grace unto thy head,
And chains about thy neck.

My son, if sinners entice thee, consent thou not.
If they say, Come with us, let us lay wait for blood,

Let us lurk privily for the innocent without cause:
Let us swallow them up alive as the grave;
And whole, as those that go down into the pit:
We shall find all precious substance,
We shall fill our houses with spoil:
Cast in thy lot among us; let us all have one purse.

My son, walk not thou in the way with them;
Refrain thy foot from their path;
For their feet run to evil,
And make haste to shed blood.

Surely in vain the net is spread in the sight of any bird.
And they lay wait for their own blood;
They lurk privily for their own lives.
So are the ways of everyone that is greedy of gain;
Which taketh away the life of the owners thereof.
Proverbs 1:2-19

AT THE PRESENT TIME, there are over one million teen-agers in America who have criminal records of one kind or another. This suggests that some 5% or more of our teen-agers have been involved in a confrontation with the police. It is probably true that only a small percentage of those are becoming hardened criminals. The majority of those million plus teen-agers were undoubtedly drawn into incriminating situations by that smaller minority which represents the WRONG CROWD. Unfortunately, that fact does not make them any less guilty in the eyes of justice.

Since each member of the human race is endowed at birth with a sinful nature, and inevitably some percentage of people are going to capitulate to this nature, there always will be wrong crowds. The "wrong crowd" acts as a test for the "right crowd." Almost any person likes to involve as many of his companions as possible in his chosen actions. For a sinner that assuages his individual guilt feelings. Consequently, (1) the wrong crowd is always on the lookout for someone who will succumb to its enticements, and (2) the right crowd should be *active* in warning and in enlightening the unwary teen-ager.

As was pointed out in Chapter II, "Prologue to Proverbs," the adolescent is a ready target for enticement because he is in a transition period, and often in a low point of his spiritual life. The only way to compensate for this natural weakness is to train young people, first of all to recognize the wrong crowd, and secondly, to have the knowledge and inner strength to resist it. An excellent means of training and preparing is through the teaching of Proverbs. For instance, they might be read and discussed in a family devotional period following the evening meal, when usually all of the family members are cheerful and relaxed. Teen-agers usually do not like to concentrate for long periods of time on lengthy dissertations. But they do respond to short, quick, illustrative pitches of wisdom such as those contained in the proverbs.

The purpose of the Book of Proverbs is set forth in the following verse,

> *To know wisdom and instruction;*
> *To perceive the words of understanding;*
> *To receive the instruction of wisdom,*
> *Justice and Judgment and Equity.*
> *To give subtilty to the simple,*
> *To the young man knowledge and discretion.*
> *Proverbs 1:2-4*

The primary purpose of proverbs is to teach WISDOM. The word "wisdom" here is the Hebrew word *chokmah* which means to point repeatedly at something, or in this context, to repeat doctrine until it is learned, first as academic knowledge and then as applied principle. Since very few people learn by hearing a thing only once, repetition is the most basic principle in teaching. The word "instruction" is the Hebrew word *musar* and connotes teaching or training by discipline. Parents must shape children's behavior by exercising authority. "Wisdom" is doctrine taken willingly into the mentality by people who are on positive volition* toward the things of God. Wisdom, when positively accepted, will help to shape the mental attitude of the receiver.

"Instruction," on the other hand, is aimed at people with negative volition* toward doctrine. They need someone over them in the chain-of-command who will force them to learn doctrine and use it to regulate their lives. In other words, "instruction" is giving children what is good for them whether they want it or not. When enforced proper behavior reaps positive dividends, the unwilling child becomes convinced of the value of following divine viewpoint. Therefore, parents have two basic responsibilities according to Proverbs. First they should teach Bible doctrine repeatedly. Secondly, they should enforce divine viewpoint when necessary, being confident that they are teaching their children how to gain, not lose, in life.

Children who submit to authoritative training at home usually go on to become successful adults. The family unit is the most basic unit of authority in society. If a child does not learn to respect parental authority, he will not respond properly to authority in other areas of his life, such as at school or at work. Most juvenile delinquents have parents who exhibited little or no concerned discipline or training. Parents do not owe their children an abundance of material possessions. Anything material the parents provide can be found also with the wrong crowd. But the precious and unique gift of every parent to his child should be *Bible doctrine*. The child who has this inheritance will be well-equipped to accumulate the material details of life through his own efforts, but he will also be equipped to have mastery over them, which is the only way to really enjoy them.

In the second line of verse 2, we have the phrase "to perceive the words of understanding." The infinitive "to perceive" in Hebrew is the word *bin* which means to get answers from your own mind. "Understanding" is the noun form of that word, *binah*. Understanding is knowledge stored in the mind for ready use. This might also be described as the individual's *frame of reference**. The person who has perception and a store of knowledge to draw upon will be self-sustaining and self-governing when a critical situation arises.

In verse 3, we have the infinitive "to receive" which in Hebrew is *lachach*, meaning to pass on. Here it teaches parents to pass on Bible doctrine to children. Parents are to pass on the instructions of wisdom which are "justice, and judgment and equity," three expressions of wisdom. "Justice" refers to the overt behavior pattern. If a person has wisdom, he will exhibit righteous behavior in accordance with divine norms and standards. "Judgment" is the expression of wisdom through the mentality, the decisions that he makes will be fair and just, in accordance with divine viewpoint. "Equity" is the expression of wisdom through character, personal integrity. These three qualities are the external evidences of a wise mind.

In verse 4, we find a categorization which recognizes that all children do not have an equal learning capacity. Bible doctrine teaches the simple to be subtle. The "simple" here are younger children who have yet to go beyond the point of babyhood as far as their spiritual progress is concerned. "Subtlety" is a cleverness of the mind that enables correct and beneficial decisions to be made. The "young man" is the teen-ager who should be more mature than a child. "Knowledge" is categorized resource material in his mentality. "Discretion" is the ability to choose from this source information to make correct decisions. If a child is taught "subtlety" while he is very young, by the time he reaches his teens, he should be capable of making wise decisions on his own.

Verses 5 and 6 form an integral tetrastich (a four-line poem), and describe again what kind of a person is developed by the teaching of Bible doctrine. With a multiplicity of such young persons, eventually a stable society is established.

> *A wise man will hear, and will increase in learning;*
> *And a man of understanding shall attain unto wise*
>   *counsels,*
> *To understand a proverb and the interpretation,*
> *The words of the wise and their dark sayings.*
> *Proverbs 1:5-6*

A wise man is the first to realize how little he really knows. He is not too proud to learn from another wiser person. He will direct his feet toward the location where he can increase his knowledge, and he will be willing to listen (on positive volition). He is eager to "understand a proverb and the interpretation." This means willingness to exert the effort of deep study necessary to research and discover the literal meanings of scriptures, thus avoiding confusion and false doctrines. In the case of mining the riches of the Book of Proverbs, it includes a discernment of the proverb's interpretation, a recognition of the abstract doctrine revealed in the figurative language.

Doctrine of Authority

In verses 7 through 9, David describes the doctrine of authority for teen-agers to recognize and follow,

> *The fear of the Lord is the beginning of knowledge,*

But fools despise wisdom and instruction.
My son, hear the instructions of thy father,
And forsake not the law of thy mother;
For they shall be an ornament of grace unto thy head,
And chains about thy neck.
Proverbs 1:7-9

The first two verses give the two basic sources of authority over the child, the Word of God and the parents. The "fear of the Lord" in Hebrew is *yirah* which means a reverential awe of God. This involves putting Christ first among your mental occupations. Whatever your mind is occupied with most frequently is what you will take time to learn most about. Therefore, to be reverentially occupied with God will lead to a life of learning and applying the Word of God. The "fool" in line 2 is the person who will not apply his knowledge. He despises doctrine. The word "despise" is *buz* which means to tread on or to kick. Fools are just that disrespectful to Bible doctrine. No one wants to be a fool, so the first authority one should submit himself to is the Word of God.

The second authority is "thy father and . . . thy mother." Notice that the word "instruction" in verse 8 is plural. There are many categories of knowledge to be learned from parents, everything from how to manage money to the choosing of a mate to the recognition and avoidance of the wrong crowd. Notice also that neither parent has a monopoly on training children.

The mother teaches the "law"; the prescribing of a manner of life. In so doing, she plays a primary role in the life of a child from years one through five. About the sixth year, the father begins to take on a more prominent role as the giver of "instruction." The word "instruction" implies a discipline, in this case disciplining a child in the law that has been taught by the mother. The father and mother each have their unique gifts to contribute in child-rearing, and any parent who leaves the job primarily to the other spouse is going to find something lacking in his children.

Verse 9 explains the result of the teaching advised in verse 8. "They" in line 1 refers to the principles of doctrine that are taught to the children. These principles are described in two metaphors, one involving masculine perspectives and the other feminine. The "ornament of grace" on the head is a crown, the universally recognized symbol of leadership. This is a Hebrew idiom used to describe a successful man, a leader among men. Therefore, the boy who learns doctrine will mature into a successful man.

"Chains about thy neck" are necklaces, an item that women have always used to adorn themselves. Just as a necklace will enhance a woman's natural physical beauty, so Bible doctrine will enhance her spiritual (or inner) beauty. It will enable her to succeed as a wife, a mother and a citizen. This verse implies that both daughters and sons have an equal need for Bible doctrine. This proverb implies that the way to be successful and attractive is to develop a mental attitude based on Biblical teaching, or wisdom. This is achieved by submitting to the authority of one's parents.

According to the teaching of Proverbs, the most important contribution that parents can make to the future success of their sons and daughters is not material goods, but spiritual viewpoint, not an expensive secular education but a thorough orientation and understanding of Bible doctrine.

Six Categories of Parental Teaching

There are six basic things that parents need to teach their children. The first of these is the *Principle of Self Discipline*. This should be taught first because self-discipline is a prerequisite to all further learning. Any one who is going to achieve success must learn to control his natural appetites. He must learn to choose his goals wisely, and deny certain lesser, temporary desires in hopes of achieving the greater success in the future. This ability is one of the primary distinctions between men and animals. Men are able to categorize pleasures, and think in terms of long-range goals, thus denying immediate temptations. The importance of self-discipline cannot be over-stressed since it is the key to all future accomplishments.

Secondly, children must be taught to respect the *Property* of others. They must recognize the right of ownership. They should be taught that each individual gains possessions by working for them, and no other individual has the right to damage or steal those possessions.

The third law that children must learn is respect for the *Privacy* of other people. They should learn not to intrude into conversations uninvited. They should learn not to annoy others by monopolizing their time.

A fourth law is the respect for *Life* itself. No single individual has the right to take the life of another person. This right is reserved for God, and in the extreme cases of murder, for the state, functioning under God as a "revenger." (Romans 13:1-7)

Fifthly, children need to be taught to respect the *Individual Rights* of other people, even as Christ did. Christ honored the rights of men when He inspired them but refused to coerce or force them. These principles are imbedded in our Constitution in terms described as the rights of "life, liberty and pursuit of happiness."

Finally, parents should teach their children respect for *Authority*. There are nine categories of authority which should be explained to the child. The first is the authority of (1) the *Word of God*, which is, indirectly, the authority of God Himself. The Word of God teaches the basis for all other areas of bona fide authority. For instance, the Bible says, "Honor thy father and thy mother," (Deuteronomy 5:16) so the next category of authority is the authority of (2) the *parents*. A child must learn this before he can learn much more from his parents. The child must then learn to respect the authority of (3) *teachers*, particularly any person who teaches the Word of God. This could be his parents, pastor, or his Sunday school teacher.

Furthermore in the area of the local church, a child must heed the authority of (4) the *official ruling board of the church*, deacons or elders. Similarly, the child must respect (5) the *rules and rulers of the State*, the law and those men who enforce it such as judges and policemen. They must recognize the authority of (6) *teachers* in the secular areas of life, such as the coach or the public school teacher. They must respect the authority of (7) the *military*, both its legal right of conscription and its internal hierarchy of authority if they are a member of the military forces. They must respect those men in authority (8) in whatever *business* they may be involved, i.e., the "boss." Finally, children should respect (9) every other *individual's authority over his own life*.

Individual volition is the first Divine Institution and although it is frequently the downfall of man (as in the case of Adam), it is also his chief dignity. Children must honor every other man's right to express his volition in determining how he will live his own life. No man has the right to express his own volition to the detriment of others. If and when he does, it is not the individual's prerogative to punish the offender, but rather it is the prerogative of the State in compliance with common law, and the State should and ought to be "under God" as is expressed in our Pledge of Allegiance.

Defining the Wrong Crowd

Perhaps it is time now to remind the reader of the chapter title, "The Enticement of the Wrong Crowd," about which little has been said thus far. At this point, we can loosely define the "wrong crowd" as anyone who rejects the principles outlined in the preceding several paragraphs, persons who reject authority and who desecrate the rights of men. Verse 10 is the preliminary alerting or warning against these kind,

My son, if sinners entice thee,
Consent thou not.
Proverbs 1:10

"Sinners" are those who delight in sin, and the tearing down of authority instituted by God. Some make it their primary occupation. The word "entice" in Hebrew is written here in the piel stem which intensifies the verb. Enticement is pressure, and hence in the piel stem, an intense pressure put upon the person.

The wrong crowd has many pressure systems. They can make an appeal to conformity which usually is hard for the teen-agers to resist. Teen-agers are immature and consequently insecure, so they often seek security in going along with the crowd, being a "regular guy." No teen wants to be a "square" or not "with it." He may be accused of being "old-fashioned" if he fails to go along with the "new morality" which entices with the suggestion that "everything is only relative." A teen-ager's crowd may not see their act as being very sinful relative to other people's behavior, but a Christian teen-ager knows that his conduct is always being viewed according to the absolute righteousness of God.

If a teen-ager quite properly hesitates, the wrong crowd might also accuse him of cowardice. They might jeer at him, such as "You're a chicken if you don't go with us to break into this store." At this point, turning one's back to their challenge, and walking away from their evil enticement would take genuine courage. Conformity is one form of cowardice.

Another weak point with teen-agers is in the area of the opposite sex. They are painfully conscious of their image in that regard. A teen-age girl might be taunted by the false threat that boys will think she is a prude if she does not lower her standards to the level of the wrong crowd. One may even be threatened with ostracism by members of one's own sex in certain cases.

Other approaches by the wrong crowd will attempt to soothe the conscience by promising protection from detection. "Don't worry. We won't get caught." They neglect to recognize God from whom nothing is hidden. (Hebrews 4:13)

Yet another enticement by the wrong crowd is the appeal to experimentation. "Don't knock it until you've tried it." As long as the teen-ager has the Word of God to guide him, he hardly needs to try something to find out if it is "right" or "wrong." He can put his trust in an authority that has outlasted every wrong crowd in history.

Loyalty to one's friends is a universal virtue, but the wrong crowd's loyalty is questionable, as is the value of their friendship. Nevertheless, the wrong crowd appeals to these principles, friendship and loyalty, "Some friend you are!" Loyalty to earthly friends should never transcend obedience to God. These enticements are often strong as well as subtle. It is often difficult to analyze and recognize them, and painful to resist them. But the rewards are worth the effort. Any teen-ager who has been instructed in wisdom should be capable of such analysis and recognition, and hence should be capable of surviving the test of the wrong crowd victoriously. This is because he understands them, and hence has objectivity.

The Activities of the Wrong Crowd

In verses 11 through 16, we read and recognize some of the activities of the wrong crowd,

If they say, Come with us, let us lay wait for blood,
Let us lurk privily for the innocent without cause:
Let us swallow them up alive as the grave;
And whole, as those that go down into the pit:
We shall find all precious substance,
We shall fill our houses with spoil:
Cast thy lot among us;
Let us all have one purse:
My son, walk not thou in the way with them;
Refrain thy foot from their path;
For their feet run to evil,
And make haste to shed blood.
Proverbs 1:11-16

Here it is noticed that one of the primary occupations of the wrong crowd is violence, and sometimes just violence for its own sake. "Let us lurk privily for the *innocent without cause.*" They apparently find a thrill in assaulting someone for either little or no purpose. But notice the pronouns. *They* (plural), the cowardly many, are looking for one (singular), the "innocent." This is the wrong crowd speaking, who accuse a hesitator of cowardice. People who resort to such violent acts seldom accomplish them on their own. Usually they are cowards who draw their courage from the crowd, often a crowd of cowards. But let every young person know that a mob of people involved in a violent course of action must be considered 'one' by those in authority. Quite often, it is the least guilty in the mob who suffer. This is exemplified in revolutionary riot tactics where the young and newly-enticed take their lumps in the front lines, while the hard-core organizers, fifteen tiers back, initiate the confrontation by throwing bricks and garbage.

The second major occupation of the wrong crowd is robbery, looking for gain where they have not earned it. Related to this in verse 14 is the enticement to criminal socialism, "let us all have one purse." If any teen-ager had even the basic instruction outlined earlier, he should know enough to avoid such activity. If he has been taught respect for life and property, as well as for the authority of the law of the state, he should know enough to desert any companions who suggest that he break divine sanctions. Many young people do not know enough to walk away from such situations. Some are too eager for the thrill of coming events and tag along with the wrong crowd without really being sympathetic to their objectives. Others think that they can go along but not participate and therefore not lower their standards. But David warns Solomon, his teen-ager, against even tagging along. "Walk not thou in the way with them."

In verse 17, we have a perfect illustration of the activities of the wrong crowd,

> *Surely in vain the net is spread*
> *In the sight of any bird.*
> *Proverbs 1:17*

The illustration used in verse 17 refers to an ancient means employed by fowlers to catch a bird. A net was propped up with a stick and a trip mechanism, and when tripped, the net came down on the victim. Bait was placed underneath the net, and beyond the trip mechanism. A smart bird was one who could see the whole mechanism, not just the bait, and would avoid it. A dumb bird would be sufficiently attracted by the bait to overlook the net and so would be trapped. The wrong crowd, like the dumb birds, see only the bait, in this case the prospect of easy if violent gain. The activities of the wrong crowd are a trap, but a trap clearly visible to those with trained eyes. A teen-ager who heeds Bible doctrine knows that the net surely follows the bait, and justice follows the actions of the wrong crowd. The "net" in this case is entrapment, capture and punishment by duly appointed law officers. The "dumb cluck" in this case is the teen-ager enticed by the wrong crowd, the teen-ager who lacks Bible doctrine. Sadly, this is often not his own fault, but rather the faults of his parents, or even perhaps of his teachers.

The Destiny of the Wrong Crowd

Verses 18 and 19 describe the destiny of the wrong crowd,

> *And they* lay wait *for their blood;*
> *They* lurk privily *for their own lives.*
> *So are the ways of everyone that is greedy of gain;*
> *Which taketh away the life of the owners thereof.*
> *Proverbs 1:18-19*

David is not lacking in humor, and he becomes quite cynical

here. Notice that in the romanized phrases, David has taken the very words from the mouths of the wrong crowd to show just how foolish their evil bravado is. While they may brag about laying wait for blood and lurking privily for the innocent, it is only their own blood and their own lives that will eventually be forfeited. They are as foolish as they are dangerous. In verse 19, he reiterates this prophecy, i.e., thieves and murderers will always meet their reward. The evil that they do will eventually come home to them, or as another proverb describes it, "He that is greedy for gain troubleth his own house." (Proverbs 15:27)

The wrong crowd is a constant menace; everyone is subject to its enticements. The unfortunate thing is that many ignorant teen-agers cannot see the net suspended above the bait. They are caught before they realize what has happened; and in dealings with the law, experience can be a rather harsh teacher. Only by a firm foundation in Bible doctrine will the teen-agers of today survive the appeal of the wrong crowd and become the successful adults of the future. The paramount responsibility is on the shoulders of parents. If they fulfill their teaching responsibility to their children, those children will have a head-start in fulfilling their responsibility to God and to society.

CHAPTER V

The Wisdom of Agur

The words of Agur the son of Jakeh, even the prophecy:
The man spake unto Ithiel, even unto Ithiel and Ucal,
Surely I am more brutish than any man,
And have not the understanding of a man.
I neither learned wisdom,
Nor have the knowledge of the holy.

Who hath ascended up into heaven, or descended?
Who hath gathered the wind in his fists?
Who hath bound the waters in a garment?
Who hath established all the ends of the earth?
What is his name, and what is his son's name, if thou
*   canst tell?*
Every word of God is pure:
He is a shield unto them that put their trust in him.
Add thou not unto his words, lest he reprove thee,
And thou be found a liar.

Two things have I required of thee;
Deny me them not before I die:
Remove far from me vanity and lies:
Give me neither poverty nor riches;
Feed me with food convenient for me:

Lest I be full, and deny thee, and say, 'Who is the Lord?'
Or lest I be poor and steal, and take the name of my God
  in vain.
Accuse not a servant unto his master,
Lest he curse thee, and thou be found guilty.
Proverbs 30:1-10

Part I: Agur's Carnality

"The Stupidity of Solomon"

CHAPTER 30 OF PROVERBS records the wisdom of a man called
Agur. The name "Agur" means "collector" or "assembler." What
is it that Agur collects? One reading of this chapter makes it
obvious that what Agur collects is observations and wisdom, wise
sayings. The method of presentation is unique. He teaches by
illustrations in series of four, hence the lessons are called *quaternaries*. As these quaternaries are analyzed and discussed, it shall
be apparent that Agur was hardly a haphazard collector. He
organized his observations and published them in a kind of progression which increases their impact.

Many scholars claim (and this author agrees) that Agur is
merely a pseudonym for Solomon. The Jewish Talmud gives six
different names for Solomon, and one of them is Agur. Chapter 30
was written near the end of Solomon's life, and this chapter reflects his long lapse into carnality* and the ensuing bitterness
that he experienced. It also reflects his eventual rebound and his
late, but not too-late, determination to get back into fellowship*
with his Creator. For many years he had ignored the lessons of
Bible doctrine which he had learned as a youth from his father,
King David. Solomon observed his son Rehoboam, the heir apparent and now a grown man, surrounding himself with foolish companions, and becoming rebellious against God Himself. Solomon
finally realized his need to rebound. Hence he describes himself as
the "son of Jakeh," Jakeh meaning "obedience." He may be using
a pseudonym because he is ashamed of himself, or perhaps because
he felt it was good to take advantage of the names and their
meanings.

Solomon's Rebound

The words of Agur the son of Jakeh, even the prophecy:
The man spake unto Ithiel, even unto Ithiel and Ucal.
Surely I am more brutish than any man,
And have not the understanding of a man,
I neither learned wisdom, nor have the knowledge of the
*   holy.*
Proverbs 30:1-3

Verse 1 indicates that the words are Solomon's, but the actual recorders or clerks may be two other men, Solomon's editors, Ithiel and Ucal, members of Solomon's Cabinet, men who recorded the teachings for the edification of Rehoboam or others who might listen. The word translated a "prophecy" does not actually mean foretelling, but rather "forth-telling" or teaching, instruction. "The man" in line 4 is a Hebrew phrase for a mighty man or a hero. The implication is that a hero, unlike Solomon, will instruct his children or students in the secrets of *both success and failure.*

The names Ithiel and Ucal are also significant. Ithiel means "God with me," and Ucal means "I am able." This verse can illustrate a basic principle of exegesis: the scriptures have only one literal interpretation, but many applications. Hence, while this verse simply records the names of the two clerks who learned from the renowned man, it also can be expanded to suggest a deeper meaning, 'As long as *God is with me, I am able* to be a (spiritual) hero.'

In verses two and three, the elderly Solomon does not sound very much like a hero. He describes himself as "brutish," super-carnal,* more so than all the rest. He pictures himself as more of an animal than a true man. He classifies himself in the category of the depraved, the "brutish." The primary area of contrast between men and animals is in man's soulish nature; and Solomon is confessing *stupidity.* This confession is a serious and surprising thing for a man whose name has become universally symbolic for wisdom. Although our language contains idioms like "as wise as Solomon" and "the wisdom of Solomon," he insists that, at least for a major part of his adult life, he did not even have the understanding of an ordinary human being. The concept of 'barnyard morality,' and his many concubines and "wives" comes to mind. "The stupidity of Solomon" is the theme song of his newly revived spirituality, his rebound.

The mentality of a human has two facets, the perception lobe and the "norms and standards" lobe. On the perception side, a man receives data in the form of stimuli from his environment, and the measure of this lobe is in how well he can understand what he perceives. The other lobe, the "norms and standards" side, evaluates the data according to its frame of reference.* Bible doctrine builds up a frame of reference based on divine viewpoint, enabling the believer to make objective judgments. However, if the person has no doctrine, he will have human viewpoint* and hence will think subjectively. He may or may not have a high human I.Q. in his perceptive lobe. But with no divine norms and standards, one tends to become like an animal (brutish).

In verse three, Solomon reveals the cause of this long lapse into stupidity. He had ignored the academics of Bible doctrine, "knowledge," as well as its application, "wisdom." The word "holy" here is actually in the plural, "holies," and refers to God's nature, the characteristics of which are described in Chapter III, "The Wages of Wisdom."

From Solomon's example, we need to realize that no matter how great we may become, if we ignore doctrine, all that has been accomplished up to that point quickly becomes undone. When we forget doctrine, we also lose the consciousness of the significance of God's essence. God's infinite love fails to comfort us. A sense of our own frailties substitutes for an awareness of His omnipotence. Fear takes over where there was once Faith-Rest.* The loss is very great, and something is needed to take the place of the loss. That something is sublimation.

In sublimation, we turn to the details of life.* The trimmings on our Christian life suddenly become the object of our whole attention, attention formerly focused on Bible doctrine. Solomon's leading detail may have been alternately money, power and sex. He had a thousand wives but no happiness. He accumulated a treasury filled with more gold than the treasuries of any other known contemporary nation. But he overtaxed his people and they became disloyal. He inherited power over the greatest kingdom of that time, but it was quickly lost by his foolish son, a spoiled prince.

Sex, money, power . . . but still Solomon failed to find happiness. Solomon must have been trained carefully as a child, for he had a great intellect. But when his great mind operated without divine viewpoint, he found only anguish and frustration. In the Book of Ecclesiastes, his frustrations are recorded. Solomon, the 'wisest' of all men, and the most intelligent of men, found that the ultimate end of all human viewpoint is "vanity and vexation of Spirit." (Ecclesiastes 2:11) He became increasingly bitter,[1] and happiness continued to elude the man with a thousand wives, until he turned back to God.

Carnality is an interruption to an effective Christian life, but it does not mean the end of an effective Christian life. Fortunately, God knew man's weakness, and so provided the Principle of Rebound*.

Ecclesiastes expressed Solomon's overwhelming cynicism while in carnality. But here in the Book of Proverbs, he describes different kinds of thoughts, new thoughts that occupied his mind after he rebounded. He first recognized his own foolishness and then, perhaps much more importantly, he recognized the majesty and magnificence of God and His creation.[2] His search and his appreciation for God took the form of five basic questions, each beginning with an interrogative pronoun. The first four questions, he asked with a Hebrew word *me* or in English, "who." In the fifth he wants to know *ma* or in English "what."

> *Who hath ascended up into heaven, or descended?*
> *Who hath gathered the wind in his fists?*
> *Who hath bound the waters in a garment?*
> *Who hath established all the ends of the earth?*
> *What is his name, and what is his son's name, if thou*
>   *canst tell?*
> *Proverbs 30:4*

Subjects in the Old Testament are categorized in many ways. That part of the Old Testament which has reference to the coming Messiah is called the Christology. It will be noted that some of Solomon's questions, especially the first and fifth, are directed

---

[1]"The words of the Preacher (Solomon) the son of David, king of Jerusalem, Vanities of vanities, all is vanity . . . I said of laughter, it is mad, and of mirth, what doeth it . . . I got me . . . maidens, . . . and women singers . . . and whatsoever mine eyes desired I kept not from them . . . and behold all was vanity, and vexation of spirit . . . Therefore I hated life . . . yea, I hated all my labor." Portions, Ecclesiastes 1:1, 2, 2:2, 7-18.

[2]This is also the story of Job as he rebounded. See Job 38-40.

toward this Christology. The second, third and fourth are directed toward God the Creator.

The first question inquires into the nature of Phase One*, the incarnation and subsequent glorification of Jesus Christ. He realizes that he must get back to what is most basic to his faith (and to ours), personal redemption by the Son of God. The person who "ascended up into heaven, or descended" is Jesus Christ, whose glorious resurrection was anticipated by various Old Testament figures. After a Christian rebounds, the first thing he wants to do is to become occupied with Christ. Then he can crowd out of his mind all residual occupations lingering from his recent carnality. To achieve this, Solomon restudied the mechanism of Phase One* so that he might rejoice in his salvation. Question number one as well as all of the successive questions seeks a general answer: The Character of God.

Solomon's second question is an inquiry into the sovereign omnipotence of the Creator in controlling the environment or nature, here exemplified by the wind. He wants to know who causes the winds which, in Palestine, brought rain from the west in the winter season, providing a basis for agricultural productivity, and also the hot dry summer winds coming off the desert, bringing harvest season. In other words, Solomon wanted to know more about God who created the circumstances of life, planting and harvest, birth and death, fauna and flora, hot and cold. The personality behind the circumstances is much more important than any of the events themselves. When a Christian realizes this, he can rejoice no matter what particular conditions he may be experiencing at the moment. In Palestine the hot, arid summer is as necessary as winter rains for the ripening process that insures a maximum harvest.

In his third question, Solomon wonders who holds the water in abeyance for the purpose of causing rain to fall. He is discussing the water cycle, rain, runoff, and evaporation. In the hot, semi-arid Middle East, this is the same as asking about the source of prosperity. He wants to know who is behind all the grace that he sees in the bountiful Earth; who sends such blessings to the human race.

Inquiry number four is searching for the intelligence that created all things with an end in mind. Geographically this could be understood as the entire scope of our planet, the "ends of the earth." But historically it can be understood as the end of history, the purpose of the human race, the climax of man in time. It is only Bible doctrine that can give Solomon the answer to such a question, Bible doctrine such as Psalm 8,

> *O Lord our Lord, how excellent is thy name in all the*
> *earth.*
> *Psalm 8:9*

or Revelation 4 by John,

> *Thou art worthy, O Lord, to receive glory and honor and*
> *power:*
> *for thou hast created all things, and for thy pleasure they*
> *are and were created.*
> *Revelation 4:11*

In the fifth question, after he has searched out God's identity and essence, Solomon wanted more personal knowledge; he wanted to know God's name, and the name of God's son. He wanted to be able to call God "my Father," and God's son, "Jesus Christ, my Lord."

Now that Solomon has revitalized his consciousness and occupied his mind with God and His Son, the next step in Rebound is to turn his attention to God's Word, which he does in verses 5 and 6.

> *Every word of God is pure:*
> *He is a shield unto them that put their trust in him.*
> *Add thou not unto his words,*
> *Lest he reprove thee, and thou be found a liar.*
> *Proverbs 30:5-6*

In the first line, God's Word is described as being "pure," but in Hebrew the word is a verb rather than a noun, and means "is being refined." We could say "every word of God is being refined." This does not mean that the Word of God is undergoing some kind of change. As raw material, the Scriptures are immutable and intrinsically good. However, when the scripture is cycled through the mind, the human spirit, and the soul and then back to the mind of man, it becomes refined in that it gains real value. Bible doctrine, like gold lying undiscovered in some mountain or desert, has an intrinsic value. But only when it is mined and put to work in society does it fulfill its ultimate potential.

The first phrase describes the worth of the Word of God; the second phrase in verse 5 uses the term "shield," that which protects. For example, when we know the doctrine of the Essence

Box, we are able to have confidence in God's character, in His protection, and so we have Faith-Rest. Prayer takes on much more meaning when God's character is kept in the consciousness while we give thanks and praise, confess our sins, intercede or petition for others and ourselves.

Verse 6 warns against adding to God's Word. There are two sources of information for the mentality. The most important is the Word of God which we can describe as divine viewpoint. The other large area of source material is the environment in which we exist. Observations and conclusions made exclusively on the basis of the second source are often just "human viewpoint." When we bring divine viewpoint into the soul, we should include observations from our environment, but exclude human viewpoint which contradicts divine viewpoint. This is hardly to say that we should not obtain a secular education, but simply that we always need to subordinate it to divine viewpoint. We then judge and evaluate from our doctrinally-based frame of reference.

The problem with human viewpoint is that it so easily leads to mental attitude sins. It promotes faith in a man or group of men rather than in God. Since men will always mislead and misinterpret, the result of such trust can only lead to bitterness, fear, hatred or tyranny. This is why God has to reprove human viewpoint and call it "a liar" in verse 6. A liar pretends to be something he is not. By implication, anyone who claims to be a Christian, but who still lives according to human viewpoint is going to look something like a liar.

This verse could apply on a national level as well. Some nations classify themselves as Christian nations. A nation which considers itself Christian but which bases its decisions on some human viewpoint, such as world opinion, rather than on divine norms and standards is also worthy to be called a liar.

A Prayer for Solomon's Latter Years

Solomon's kingship lasted for forty years, 971-931 B.C. His reign is divided into three phases: (1) the early period during which he constructed the temple, (2) the second period, which included wine, 1000 women, and song, and (3) the third period, his rebound. The first period lasted about 15 years, the second about 20 years, and the last about 5 years.

At the time this chapter of Proverbs was written Solomon did not have many more years to live. He wrote a beautiful prayer for wisdom in the closing years of his life.

> *TWO THINGS have I required of thee;*
> *Deny them not to me before I die:*
> *Remove far from me vanity and lies;*
> *Give me neither poverty nor riches;*
> *Feed me with good convenient for me,*
> *Lest I be full, and deny thee, and say,*
>   *Who is the Lord?*
> *Or lest I be poor, and steal,*
>   *and take the name of my God in vain.*
> *Proverbs 30:7-9*

Solomon was an older man, probably in his middle sixties, when he prayed on these matters. Naturally he hoped for fulfillment before the end of his life. But this hardly means that these same requests cannot be made by a young man. How much better it would be that these conditions persist through the entire life rather than only briefly at the end. His first request is for his soul, his mental attitudes. The second request is for his body, his physical needs.

The first requirement for a healthy soul is understanding THE DOCTRINE OF VANITY. We should remember from reading Ecclesiastes that vanity was Solomon's leading song. The word for vanity in Hebrew is *shaweh,* and means three things: confusion, emptiness and worthlessness. The soul that has categorical Bible doctrine will be full. It will have order and objectivity. It will be valuable like refined gold. From Proverbs 30:6 it is learned that "lies" refer to human viewpoint. Solomon finally determined to live according to divine viewpoint so that his life would exemplify truth and not a lie.

Solomon then turns to his physical needs and gives us THE DOCTRINE OF EXCESSES. We must remember that this comes from a man who has known well the one side of excesses, the positive side. No doubt he had been a leader in organizing and producing many rich banquets. But now, on divine viewpoint, he wants "neither poverty nor riches" but rather just enough to live comfortably.

In any extreme condition, there are temptations which Solomon describes in verse 9. "Full" is an idiom for rich, and a rich man usually has difficulty in living the Christian life. Christ pointed this out in his encounter with the rich young ruler,

> *How hardly shall they that have riches (details of life)*
> *enter into the kingdom of God!*
> *For it is easier for a camel to go through a needle's eye,*
> *than for a rich man to enter into the kingdom of God.*
> *Luke 18:24-25*

The rich can afford all the details of life which so easily distract men from the ways of faith. They begin to think of themselves as entirely self-sufficient since they can quickly satisfy all physical desires. The temptation then is to think, 'Who needs God?', or as Solomon puts it, "Who is the Lord?" Wealth can be the source of a great testimony for the Christian who can manage it constructively, and say, 'Whatever I have accomplished is the work of the Lord, to God be the glory.' But such a man is a rarity. The danger for the wealthy of becoming prideful is everpresent.

Poverty is at the opposite end of the spectrum from riches. Some may quickly make the judgment that if wealth is a snare, then its opposite, poverty, must be a virtue. On the contrary, poverty may be just as dangerous since it leads to discontent, envy, or jealousy. Mental attitude sins begin when we envy others with more wealth, regardless of how they got it. From this point it is easy to escalate into an overt sin such as stealing, swindling, or robbing. Whatever the level of quick but unearned acquisition may be, it results in taking God's name in vain. This does not mean swearing, but rather blaspheming. The overt sin such as stealing reveals one's lack of belief that God can take care of us, and hence it is a kind of blasphemy against God's character of love and omnipotence. If then, we desire to isolate ourselves from the twin temptations of pride and envy, our prayer should be for enough substance as is "convenient" rather than either extreme. This is the doctrine of excess.

A "Lonesome End" Proverb[3]

This "lonesome end" proverb is not specifically related to the preceding passage except that it points out the danger of judging others, a point which Christ reiterated in the Sermon on the Mount. (Matthew 7:1)

> *Accuse not a servant unto his master,*
> *Lest he curse thee, and thou be found guilty.*
> *Proverbs 30:10*

Operating by human viewpoint, we tend to judge others rather than ourselves. Solomon judged himself, and rebounded. He then related his experience, his stupidity, and then even published it as an example to warn other believers against repeating his mistakes. Doctrine is taught to enable us to judge ourselves according to God's intent for our short stay on Earth. It is not given for us to judge others.

"Accuse not" is in the hiphil or causative stem, meaning that we are caused to become accusative by something within ourselves such as envy, hatred, or jealousy. With such sins within the heart, the soul is not able to be occupied with Christ, and so it turns its attention on other people. The result is Operation Busybody. The person who starts looking for the sins of others is going to end up accusing a fellow "servant" to their common "master," and for Christians the common master is Christ. In extreme or prolonged cases, the punishment for Operation Busybody is a threefold curse:

(1) Self-induced misery

(2) Divine discipline for the sin of judging, and

(3) Divine discipline for the sin of which the accuser judged his fellow servant. We call this *triple-compound discipline,* and it is obviously something to be avoided.

In this introduction to his quaternaries, Solomon (or Agur) has bared his own soul and thereby served as an illustration both of the dangers of carnality and the means of Rebound. He has taught us that the most important things in life are not material circumstances, i.e., "poverty nor riches," but principles of Bible doctrine. Keeping this in mind, we can now observe some of the doctrines

---

[3]This term is adapted from a football formation first employed at West Point where an end did not engage in the normal huddle, but appeared as an isolated player on the field.

which will keep us in fellowship during our few years on Earth, so that we can avoid experiencing severe lapses into carnality.

Part II: Agur's Quaternaries

A. *There is a* generation *that curseth their father,*
   And doth not bless their mother.
   There is a generation *that are pure in their own eyes,*
   And yet is not washed from their filthiness.
   There is a generation, *O how lofty are their eyes!*
   And their eyelids are lifted up.
   There is a generation *whose teeth are as swords,*
   And their jaw teeth as knives, to devour the poor from
   off the earth,
   And the needy from among men.

B. *The horseleath hath two daughters,*
   Crying, Give, give.
   There are three things that are never satisfied, *yea four*
   things say not,
   It is enough.
   The grave; *and the* barren womb;
   The earth *that is not filled with water;*
   And the fire *that saith not, It is enough.*
   The eye that mocketh at his father,
   And despiseth to obey his mother,
   The ravens of the valley shall pick it out,
   And the young eagles shall eat it.

C. *There be three things which are too wonderful for me,*
   Yea, four which I know not:
   The way of an eagle *in the air;*
   The way of a serpent *upon a rock;*
   The way of a ship *in the midst of the sea;*
   And the way of a man *with a maid.*
   Such is the way of an adulterous woman;
   She eateth, and wipeth her mouth,
   And saith, I have done no wickedness.

D. *For three things the earth is disquieted,*
  And for four which it cannot bear;
  For a servant *when he reigneth;*
  And a fool *when he is filled with meat;*
  For an odious woman *when she is married;*
  And an handmaid *that is heir to her mistress.*

E. *There be four things which are little upon the earth,*
  But they are exceeding wise:
  The ants *are a people not strong,*
  Yet they prepare their meat in the summer;
  The conies *are but a feeble folk,*
  Yet make they their houses in the rocks;
  The locusts *have no king,*
  Yet go they forth all of them by bands;
  The spider *taketh hold with her hands,*
  And is in kings' palaces.

F. *There be three things which go well,*
  Yea, four are comely in going:
  A lion *which is the strongest among beasts,*
  And turneth not away for any,
  A greyhound, *an* he goat *also:*
  And a king *against whom there is no rising up.*
  Proverbs 30:11-31

Verses 11 through 31 of Proverbs 30 are written in *quaternaries,* or groups of four items, compared to illustrate a principle. The nature of the metaphors are various, quite frequently animals. But the technique of communication is vivid and effective.

Progressive National Decline

Quaternary A
The Case of the Four Decadent Generations

There is a generation that curseth their father,
  And doth not bless their mother.   (Generation 1)
There is a generation that are pure in their own eyes
  And yet are not washed from their filthiness.   (Generation 2)

> *There is a generation, Oh how*
> *Lofty are their eyes!*   (Generation 3)
> *There is a generation, whose teeth*
> *are like swords,*   (Generation 4)
> *And their jaw teeth as knives,*
> *To devour the poor from off the earth,*
> *And the needy from among men.*
> *Proverbs 30:11-14*

This quaternary teaches us the frightening fact that it only requires four decadent generations in succession to totally destroy a
nation or a civilization. The four successive generations described
above follow each other in a natural, causative progression; one
decadent generation tends to breed another increasingly decadent
one.

The First Decadent Generation

The first decadent generation loses respect for their parents and,
consequently, for other forms of authority. The parent is the most
natural figure to obey, and if a child fails to learn obedience to his
parents, he can hardly be expected to obey other authorities else-
where. Thus the survival of any society depends upon the mainten-
ance of the family unit and the chain-of-command and respect
therein.

The word "curseth" in verse 11 is in the piel or intensive active
stem, and the tense is present linear. This generation, then, not
just occasionally, but rather *habitually and intensively* rejects their
fathers' words, treats the father, the chief symbol of authority to a
child, with disrespect, and fails to bless the mother. A child blesses
his mother by listening to her advice, suggestions and commands,
by desiring to obey, by respecting her teachings, and by following
her example. This first verse is the prototype of all rebellion since
the parents are the earliest and the primary form of authority for
the teenager. This first verse is also the prototype of rebellion for
all the successive decadent generations, since they all deal with
some form of rejection of authority which God has authorized.[4]

---

[4]"Honour thy father and thy mother: that thy days may be long upon the
land which the Lord thy God giveth thee." Exodus 20:12 (See also Ephesians
6:1-4)

This is a superficial symptom of a deeper rejection, that of God Himself.

The Second Decadent Generation

The second decadent generation, somewhat worse, is the unjust and self-righteous crowd. They think of themselves as "pure," special or somehow superior ("pure in their own eyes"). They disregard divine viewpoint altogether. When an individual rejects the authority of his parents, and at the age of discretion when a teenager rejects the authority of God, he becomes his own authority. He rationalizes his actions and justifies his goals simply in terms of his own personal norms and standards, his own ambitions and goals, often originated in his Old Sin Nature*. This is subjectivity. Each individual sees himself or herself as the central figure of the universe, a childish outlook. This condition tends toward anarchy which can only be solved via more human viewpoint, i.e., by tyranny. God's view of such "superior" people is that they are not washed, filthy. This is a reference to the depravity of the Old Sin Nature that is not controlled and limited by Bible doctrine. Doctrine is a form of authority, but it is useless to people who assume that they have only themselves to answer.

The phrase "not washed" covers two of the three categories of mankind, (1) the unsaved, and (2) Christians in carnality, persons out of fellowship and to some degree dominated by their Old Sin Nature. This generation has very few spiritual people, although it may have many Christians living in general carnality. The third category of mankind is the "salt of the earth," believers living in fellowship under the dynamic equation*.

There are two kinds of sanctification. Ironically, both are lacking in this generation which considers itself "pure," i.e., self-righteous. The first is *positional sanctification* which is needed by the first group, the unsaved. This group has not had its sins "washed" by the blood (atonement) of Jesus Christ, and so its position is still in the world rather than in Christ. The second sanctification is *experiential sanctification*. When we sin after we are saved, we lose our fellowship with the Lord, as well as our ability to produce divine good, hence the need for Rebound or confession of our sins which places us back into fellowship. This then is a moment by moment sanctification and Christians who remain in carnality and do not confess their sins lack experiential sanctification. As part of the generation that thinks itself "pure," they will see no need to confess or rebound, and so will only aid further in the destruction of the society, be it a nation or an entire civilization.

The Third Decadent Generation

The third decadent generation is a result of no rebound in the second generation. It is described by an idiom which refers to complete and thorough pride, "how lofty are their eyes . . . their eyelids are lifted up." Human viewpoint reigns supreme; it is a result of the previous generation's accumulation of sin. The self-righteousness of the second generation leads to much arrogance and pride in the third generation. From pride comes a particularly dangerous lust pattern called *Human Approbation Lust*. The proud man seeks to please first himself and secondly other men, but never God. He may endeavor to impress men by his intelligence, his possessions, his prowess, his wealth or whatever he thinks will best gain the approbation (approval) of others. An intensification of this lust then develops in an endeavor to coerce other men, a somewhat explosive condition. Those men who are "lofty in their own eyes" are also intolerant of divine viewpoint. This condition is always a *prime danger signal;* Proverbs has warned that:

> *Pride goeth before destruction,*
> *And an haughty spirit before a fall.*
> *Proverbs 16:18*

It is natural therefore that even as the third decadent generation precedes the fourth decadent generation, so pride precedes destruction; an haughty or lofty spirit goeth before a fall. History provides many examples.

The Fourth Decadent Generation

The fourth decadent generation may not appear to be decadent since it possesses wealth, prowess, impressive talk, and the like. But all appearances aside, it is arrogant, insensitive, unteachable and stupid, and in reality it is in peril. It feeds its well-developed pride lust with cruel power; their "teeth are as swords." Their words are cruel and their deeds are cruel. The "poor . . . and needy" are people who are not capable of defending themselves.

Such helpless people are abused and taken advantage of and even consumed by the power-hungry.

Communism serves as a leading example. Communists' "teeth are as swords." Their deeds are like knives, harming millions of helpless victims. In order to maintain a facade of technical progress and an extravagant life style for a small clique of high ranking leaders, Communism robs the masses of hard-earned profits, and then boasts of its supposed concern for labor. Interestingly enough, it tolerates NO Bible doctrine. Dictatorship and tyranny, whether in a blatant form as in the case of Nazi Germany, or in a form hidden behind a smoke screen of charitable-sounding propaganda and a prison-like Iron Curtain, is the logical result of the four decadent generations.

What originates as a self-righteous rebellion, dominated by collective old sin natures, ends up in widespread cruelty, violence and tyranny. There is a generation that curseth its father and mother. There is a generation that is pure in its own eyes. There is a generation, how lofty are their eyes. There is a generation whose teeth are as swords and knives. And there is a generation in this 20th Century which needs to understand this.

Quaternary B
The Case of the Four Insatiables
Social Parasites

The horseleach hath two daughters,
Crying, give, give.
There are three things that are NEVER SATISFIED,
Yea, four things say not, It is enough.
The grave and the barren womb,   (Insatiables 1 and 2)
The earth that is not filled with water;   (Insatiable 3)
And the fire that sayeth not, It is enough.   (Insatiable 4)
Proverbs 30:15-16

The four insatiables are all members of and leaders of the four decadent generations. Their lust patterns, under the governing of their old sin natures, are never satisfied, and can never be satisfied until the destruction of the society is achieved. The more they get, the more they want. Conversely, the less they get, the less troublesome, i.e., more manageable, they are.

The word "horseleach" does not actually appear in the Hebrew language. Their word *aluquah*, here translated "horseleach," refers to two possible things, one animal and one spiritual. They are (1) a bloodsucker or vampire, and (2) a demon. The vampire has an insatiable thirst for human blood, as does the bloodsucker. A demon is never satisfied until it has gained control in a human body. The *aluquah* then is the class or group of parasites in a generation or in a nation who will plague it, prey on it, and seek to dominate and absorb all of its life. Instead of working for support in nature, parasites, such as leaches, maintain themselves from the strength and work of others and produce nothing of value. The *aluquah* or leach is a proverbial example of the social parasite who chooses to live off the labor and profits of others rather than to work constructively within society. They say, 'Give us what you have, and if you don't give us enough, we will take what we want.' Again socialists come to mind, leaders lacking divine viewpoint, and imposing increasing degrees of tyranny.

Here four inanimate things are given a personality to illustrate the nature of the social parasite. The first is the grave which, as long as life goes on, will never be full. The second is the barren womb which never stops craving a child. The barren womb keeps saying, 'Give me children', and the grave keeps saying, "Give me bodies."

The third example is the earth or parched ground. In certain parts of semi-arid Palestine such as the Negev and the Jordan Valley annual rainfall may be as low as 4 inches per year and the evaporation potential is great. The soil is ever parched, and when rain comes, even much rain, is never saturated, or satisfied. Even when irrigated water is poured out on the desert, it is soaked up immediately and within a few minutes the desert would cry again, 'Water, water!'

The fourth insatiable is a fire which forever craves fuel. A fire will feed upon and destroy everything in sight until it is isolated or destroyed by quenching. The impersonal character of a fire is to constantly demand more. It is the personal character of insatiable parasites also to constantly demand more.

The best answer to the grave is faith in Christ, who in resurrection conquered the grave. The best answer to the insatiables, the social parasites, is the Christian faith. The best answer to the barren womb is spiritual birth, which is synonymous with salvation. The best answer to the parched land is a new climate; so also the best answer for the social parasite is a climate of Bible doctrine, providing an entirely new orientation. The best answer to the fire is isolation, and Bible doctrine isolates rather than feeds the old sin nature*. Thus, Bible doctrine, is the key to the problem of the four decadent generations.

Spiritual renewal is the prescription for the insatiables. If these citizens can replace their illegitimate lusts with spiritual values, they will become occupied with Christ. Therein they will for the first time find genuine satisfaction. Then such Bible doctrine as Hebrews 13:5 takes on an expanded meaning.

Let your conversation be without covetousness,
And be content with such things as ye have.

A Second Lonesome End Proverb

The eye that mocketh at his father,
And despiseth to obey his mother,
The ravens of the valley shall pick it out,
And the young eagles shall eat it.
Proverbs 30:17

The teenager who consistently rejects parental authority will soon reject other wider forms of authority such as civil law and principles of health. He will perhaps get his kicks out of drugs until his youthful body becomes derelict. Or perhaps he will make an adventure of crime and die in violence. When ravens assume charge of a carcass, they just happen to start with the eyes, and eagles characteristically feed on carrion also. Here Solomon resorts to what might be called a scare technique; yet there are teenagers who do learn from such methods. Some of them do get the message.

Quaternary C
The Case of the Four Perilous Attacks
Social Predators

In verses 18 and 19, Solomon describes four perilous attacks.

The fourth perilous attack is repeated by verse 20 in an alternate version.

> *There are three things which are too wonderful for me,*
> *Yea four which I know not:*
> *The way of an* eagle *in the air,*   (Attack 1)
> *The way of a* serpent *upon a rock*   (Attack 2)
> *The way of a* ship *in the midst of the sea;*   (Attack 3)
> *And the way of a* man with a maid.   (Attack 4a)
> *Such is the way of an* adulterous woman;   (Attack 4b)
> *She eateth and wipeth her mouth,*
> *And saith, I have done no wickedness.*
> *Proverbs 30:18-20*

A characteristic of the parasite as seen in the preceding quaternary, Quaternary B, is a very slow but steady destruction, not involving drama or violence. A characteristic of the predator, on the other other hand, is the sudden and surprise attack, equally deadly when successful. With a parasite, patience is a necessary quality. With a predator, stalking is a necessary quality. A teenager on human viewpoint is more likely to be attracted to the social predator, because he likes excitement and risky activities such as drug experimentation, pre-marital sex experimentation, unearned property acquisition. Adults, less excitable and more wary, are more likely to be attracted to social parasitism.

The first three attacks each illustrate characteristics of the fourth. This is *speed* in the case of the eagle, *subtlety* in the case of the serpent and *surprise* in the case of the pirate ship. When Solomon describes these attacks as "wonderful," he is not being complimentary. He simply means that they are beyond his comprehension, and in a sense unpredictable. Since they happen so quickly, they are difficult to anticipate; hence to be forewarned is to be forearmed.

The first attacker is the eagle who swoops out of the sky with great speed and accuracy to collect his prey. He has sharp eyes and can locate a small rodent from up in the sky. He can dive and catch it without touching the ground, and therefore his attack leaves no tracks.

The second predator is the snake lying on a rock. Well-camouflaged by his coloring, his silence, and his stillness; he is nearly invisible. Once a victim comes within range, the snake strikes so quickly that to avoid the attack is difficult if not impossible.

The third example is a pirate ship which suddenly appears from out of nowhere, strikes, and sails off again, possibly into the fog. As with the air and the rocks, the water also retains no tracks. The victim is suddenly taken and the predator is difficult to follow or apprehend. To what common object are all of these animal predators analogous in society? "The way of a man with a maid."

Young, adventure-loving teenage girls without Bible doctrine are easy prey for experienced, fast-talking young men who move swiftly. As destructive as an eagle, a snake or a rapacious pirate ship, these youthful predators may not take a girl's life, but they will surely try to take her innocence. Instead of leaving behind a dead body, as in the case of the animal predators, they may well leave behind an extra body, very much alive, very much needing parental authority and Bible doctrine — an illegitimate child. A rodent needs to appraise all directions in order to avoid the eagle from one direction or the snake from another. A merchant ship embarking on a long voyage arms itself and posts lookouts against attacking pirate ships. A young maid with Bible doctrine will arm herself, not with physical weapons but with spiritual weapons, knowledge, understanding and discretion. She proceeds with forethought at all times.

There is a balance struck in this quaternary, for Solomon is not content to make men the sole illustrations of such villainy. In verse 20, he reminds young teenage men that there are also some perverse ladies to note and avoid, the adulterous woman. "Wipeth her mouth" had the same implication then as now; the appetite has been satisfied temporarily. This woman goes gaily from one affair to another, seducing vulnerable young men. Since none of them really mean much to her, she can easily wipe her hands of them and rationalize to herself that she has done nothing wrong. Teenagers fall prey to such activity if they are (a) lacking Bible doctrine, (b) bored, (c) rebellious, or (d) unemployed. Parents can avoid these circumstances if they keep their teenager busy in a worthwhile, constructive activity such as contributing to the family needs, and if they keep him respectful of authority. A busy mind and body are the best deterents to the idleness which can so easily lead to preoccupation with sensual, rebellious thoughts.

This does not mean that a child must become a slave to his parents; he is to respect all forms of authority. He may keep busy not only by fulfilling certain responsibilities (chores) at home, but also by participating in outside activities that are fun as well as healthy. This might include sports programs, scouting groups and part-time jobs. A busy and respectful youngster hardly leads a dull life; he learns self-respect and simultaneously he edifies others. Parents must first gain the respect of their teenager and then use their influence to encourage him toward constructive, healthy, rewarding activities. Most important, however, is to teach him respect for the authority of God's Word which in turn can give him the self-discipline and the resources to motivate himself.

Quaternary D
The Case of the Four Trouble Makers
Unqualified Leadership

Our fourth quaternary describes four people who become trouble-makers by failing to govern their lives with Bible doctrine. It is particularly unfortunate when they become leaders in society. Like the social parasites and the social predators, the social trouble-makers are an essential ingredient in the four decadent generations.

> *For three things the earth is disquieted,*
> *And for four which it cannot bear:*
> *For a* servant *when he reigneth;*   (Trouble-Maker 1)
> *And a* fool *when he is filled with meat;*   (Trouble-Maker 2)
> *For an* odious *woman when she is married;*   (Trouble-Maker 3)
> *And an* handmaid *when she is heir to her mistress.*
>   (Trouble-Maker 4)
>
> *Proverbs 30:21-23*

"Disquieted" in verse 21 means disturbed, and "cannot bear" in the second line actually means "cannot endure." Trouble-makers tend not only to disturb a society, but in the end also tend to destroy it. A similarity between all four cases can be noticed; all four trouble-makers are put in positions of leadership for which they are unprepared. An alternate title for this quaternary might be "The Four Unqualified Leaders." No nation or social group can survive without capable leadership. Leadership needs to have imagination, knowledge, perception, responsiveness and self-control.

The first trouble-maker is a "servant," perhaps a slave who, through some quirk of fate, "reigneth," finds himself in a position of leadership. He is not trained to rule, although training alone does not make a good ruler. A good leader must have all the qualities mentioned in the preceding paragraph. In addition he must realize that his function is to work for the benefit of the majority. A servant, untrained in the responsibility of, and lacking the perspective of leadership, will most likely betray trust and do just what is most beneficial to himself. He will tend to become a tyrant. A particularly poor kind of leader is the "self-server." When these types are numerous in national leadership the civilization is in danger.

The second trouble-maker is the fool who has suddenly become wealthy, "filled with meat," perhaps through an inheritance. A fool normally decreases rather than increases an inheritance. For instance, if he is bequeathed a business, he will not manage the business well. Rather than making sound developments and investments, he will probably squander his money on luxuries which lose both their appeal and their value very quickly. The economic prosperity which a nation enjoys cannot survive long under the management of such fools. A reading of subsequent Hebrew history suggests that Solomon's son, Rehoboam, in urging an increased tax load on an already overtaxed populace, illustrates this kind of trouble-maker. The result, a reaction to overtaxation in that case, was a civil war from which Judah never recovered. Rehoboam, a fool, took advice from his spoiled youthful cronies rather than from older, more experienced, more compassionate men.

The "servant" and the "fool" are examples of male trouble-makers. But Solomon is not one to overlook either sex. The third and fourth trouble-makers are of the female variety. The "odious woman" of verse 23 is one who has a bad disposition, and likes contention. This case applies particularly to leadership within the family, the basic social group of a nation. A leadership problem arises within the family when the woman attempts to assume leadership for the entire family, a position for which she is not created, but a position which she may lust after. No woman is qualified as the leader of any family as long as the husband is present. The word "odious" in Hebrew is *sana* which implies mental ugliness, a sinful mental attitude. It would be marvelously convenient if all women who were mentally ugly were physically ugly as well, but unfortunately God did not choose to make life quite that easy. He expects a man to use his mind as well as his aesthetic sense in choosing a woman who will share his life and care for his children. God's chain-of-command for the family is for the wife to *obey* the husband *whether or not* the husband follows Christian teaching.

The unmarried woman as well as the married woman makes her appearance in verse 23. She is the last member in this quartet of trouble-makers, the handmaiden who is "heir to her mistress." A handmaiden is usually a servant who has been given a somewhat elevated position. When she is suddenly promoted to the role of mistress, she becomes arrogant and haughty, and abuses the other handmaidens under her new found authority. She may well use her position to hurt certain of those ladies who are suddenly under her. She too is totally unprepared for leadership, particularly in the spiritual sense.

This quaternary teaches us an important principle. Only those people who are unselfish, qualified and deserving should be given positions of leadership. Despite the fact that all people are equal in the eyes of the law, we must recognize that all are not equal in ability or attitude. This does not mean that a mistress is better than her handmaid, but only that her position is different in the chain-of-command. Leadership needs to be awarded on a basis of training, which includes a good record of performance in lesser duties. Whether we are choosing deacons for our local church, executives for our corporation, teachers for our institutions of learning or political representatives, we must always keep in mind the principle that leadership is the key to the success of any social group. When leadership fails, the people fail with it. This is the over-all story of the four decadent generations.

The scriptures often go from the negative to the positive, such as the fall of mankind to the restoration of mankind, the trial of Job to the triumph of Job, the crucifixion of our Lord to the resurrection. Whether by coincidence or design, the quaternaries of Proverbs 30 also go from the negative to the positive. Four negative principles have been examined in the four decadent generations, the four insatiables, the four perilous attacks and the four trouble-makers. We now proceed, happily, to first the four small successes and from there to the four great successes.

Progressive National Decline

Quaternary E
The Case of the Four Small Successes
Smallness and Success

This fifth quaternary uses examples from the animal kingdom, and therein chooses four 'little folk' to serve as metaphors for successful Christian living.

> *There be four things which are little upon the earth,*
> *But they are exceeding wise:*
> *The* ants *are a people not strong,*   (Small success 1)
> *Yet they prepare their meat in the summer;*
> *The* conies *are but a feeble folk,*   (Small success 2)
> *Yet make they their houses in the rocks;*
> *The* locusts *have no king,*   (Small success 3)
> *Yet go they forth all of them by bands;*
> *The* spider *taketh hold with her hands,*   (Small success 4)
> *And is in kings' palaces.*
> *Proverbs 30:24-28*

A small success is of course much better than a grand failure, as were some of the earlier examples. To be successful in the Christian life, we need to admit our own smallness. Pride and conceit never make it in God's program. If God has greater designs for you later, He will provide the means for greatness apart from what you are inherently. (James 4:10, I Peter 5:6) Religion, which is man working and God supposedly receiving, is not the key to success. The secret is grace, which is God working and man receiving. God provides Divine Operating Assets* which we can utilize as we stay in fellowship. However, His grace assets have four enemies which need to be recognized and avoided.

The first enemy of grace is *Legalism,* the do-it-yourself religious approach, often found in fundamentalist circles. Legalism is religion without grace. Legalism tries to please God through a strict adherence to a series of arbitrary taboos, an arrogant "I don't drink and smoke and chew, and I don't run with the boys who do" attitude. Christ, the Saviour of mankind, was challenged by the legalistic crowd for being a companion of tax-collectors and harlots. His purpose, however, was to display maximum grace to these unhappy people. Legalism quickly forgets that the Bible puts only one condition on salvation — faith. Faith is the only thing that pleases grace. Faith and grace form a true and lasting spiritual marriage, beginning at the point of salvation and continuing throughout the Christian Life. (Colossians 2:6, II Corinthians 5:7)

The second enemy of grace is *Emotionalism*. A person who governs his life according to how he feels will never be able to appropriate the divine operating assets. There are a multitude of reasons why you may not feel good at any given time, but very few of them are related to your spirituality.

The third enemy of grace is *Sincerity*. Sincerity often leaves a person open to Satanic delusion. A person may be extremely sincere, but if he completely neglects or rejects Bible doctrine, he can be sincerely mistaken. The answers to successful Christian living are in God's Word, not in the delusion known as 'sincerity' which can be completely lacking in knowledge or direction.

The fourth hindrance to grace is *Human Viewpoint*. Human viewpoint encompasses everything from atheism and animism to sophisticated modern existentialism. Its universal characteristic is rejection and often ignorance of Bible doctrine. The only way to lead a victorious Christian life is to utilize grace assets, and the *only* responder to grace is faith, not any system of human philosophy. The four little creatures in Quaternary E exemplify *the nature of faith*.

All of the creatures of this quaternary are small, and therefore are vulnerable. Christians are also vulnerable, but they, like those little animals, must possess traits which will enable them to survive and succeed in a hostile world. None of these little animals would be a match for the predators of their environment if it were not for God's special provisions (instincts) for each of them. Similarly, the Christian possesses the instinct of faith in God but because of the retention of his Old Sin Nature, he remains quite vulnerable to the world, the flesh and the devil unless he appropriates the divine operating assets provided by God. Each of the following animals illustrates one of these special assets that God has made available to believers.

THE ANT. In verse 25 we meet the ant. His means of survival

are intelligent and timely preparations for the hardships of the future. Since he is "not strong," the ant could not survive the winter if he had to venture out into the cold daily to forage for food. Fortunately he 'knows' or senses this limitation in himself. Consequently, during the summer when the living is easy and the temptation is to play and enjoy the easy life, the ant is busily storing up enough food to last through the cold months ahead. The ant (unlike the parasite) lives for the future.

But when is the summertime of the Christian life? For most it is right now. If things are going smoothly enough so that you have time and peace of mind to sit down and read this book, then it must be summertime, time to store up some Bible doctrine for the winter ahead, the coming time of pain and pressure. It may be difficult to look outside on a warm, sunny day and imagine the sky filled with clouds or the winds whipping up a blizzard, but our instincts should tell us that such a time will likely come. When it does, we will be in no position then to absorb doctrine; we will be busy just trying to survive. In ancient Egyptian hyeroglyphics, the first translators had trouble deciphering one symbol, the picture of the ant. They finally learned that it was the symbol for wisdom. It is a marvelous world that God has created where we can learn great lessons from such a humble creature.

THE CONY. Our second teacher is the cony (coney), or the hyrax (Hyracoidea procavia). It is sometimes called a daman. It is not native to either of the American continents or Europe. It is limited to the mountains of Africa and Western Asia. It is a rodent, something like a rabbit or raccoon. It has a small fox-like head, and multiple back teeth like hooved animals.

The cony is a herbivorate, a weak and extremely vulnerable animal to such predators as the fox, the hyena, the lion or the eagle. His one defense he utilizes well; it is his home, a hole or cleft in the "rocks" where nothing so large as a fox or hyena can follow.

The Christian can quickly find just such a refuge in Jesus Christ and the access is a thorough knowledge of His Word. Here we find comfort in the doctrine of Christian suffering, we can ride out the storm in Faith-Rest. But just being a Christian does not get us into that cleft. If our minds are a vacuum, i.e., ignorant of doctrine, we may wander aimlessly, whereas the informed Christian, like the smart cony or hyrax, knows exactly where the little crack in the rock is so that he can dart in so quickly that a predator is left in total frustration.

THE LOCUST. In verse 27 our example is the locust. The locust teaches us how the individual Christian lends impact to the whole body of believers. The locusts have no leader among themselves; no one locust is considered supreme above all the rest. This does not mean that leaders are not needed in efficient administration, but it simply means that Christians should never put all their hopes in any particular man. Self-sustained believers should be the goal of any Bible ministry. The Christian should completely trust in Bible doctrine and in the Character of God. Then he can be self-sustained and work in harmony with other believers. Though our individual gifts may seem small and of little significance, when combined with the gifts of other Christians, they can be highly effective. It is well-known that an army of locusts, even without a leader, makes an enormous impact. Our goal as Christians should be to become effective and self-sustaining like the locust, though not destructive.

THE LIZARD. Verse 28 names the "spider," although the correct translation of the Hebrew should be "lizard," "the *lizard* is easy to take hold of with the hands." He is easily caught. Despite the fact that he is relatively slow and weak, the lizard is often found in the king's palace, a location symbolic of great success. If we develop the fruits of the spirit we can both have and bring to others such qualities as inner happiness, joy, peace and resourcefulness. Such attitudes are always welcome, particularly in kings' palaces. The lizard is an example of an animal which seems outwardly vulnerable, and yet is often most successful out of its natural environment, even in the environment of a palace.

Our Creator has provided every creature, no matter how small or weak, with some means of protection and survival. Every believer has a role within the body of the Church, and although it may seem minor, it is still significant. Whether it is important to be great in the eyes of men is quite debatable. Either way, however, a Christian must first be successful in God's eyes, and the secret to that success is to realize our own smallness. To this end, the quaternary just studied precedes one which deals with creatures which have become externally great. It is as if small successes may lead on occasion to greater successes.

Quaternary F
The Case of the Four Great Successes
Faith in Action

This quaternary points out that once a Christian becomes oriented to God's grace, and claims the divine operating assets, he begins to manifest an outward character of greatness to match his inner greatness. Appreciation and respect come his or her way. Paul's grace orientation was evident when he said, "I labored more abundantly than they all: yet not I: but the grace of God which was with me." (I Corinthians 15:10) Paul, whose name means *small*, recognized his own limited stature. In his smallness and in God's unfathomable wisdom, this little man became a hero in God's Plan. He founded many "little" churches, and wrote several "little" epistles. The little churches grew, and in time they framed more than a little of mankind's history.

> *There be three things which go well,*
> *Yea, four are comely in going;*
> A lion *which is strongest among beasts,*   (Great Success 1)
> *And turneth not away for any;*
> A greyhound *(war-horse); an* he-goat *also;*
>   (Great Successes 2, 3)
> *And a* king *against whom there is no rising up.*
>   (Great Success 4)
>
> *Proverbs 30:29-31*

A paraphrasing of verse 29 will make it more easily understood, 'There be three things that do well, *step by step,* yes, four are *beautiful in action.*' As is indicated by the italicized words, the emphasis in this verse (and in this quaternary) is on action, constructive action. The believer always makes more impact by what he does than by what he says. It is relatively easy to mouth Christian principles as abstract and lofty ideals, but the true test of faith is the acting out of those principles in our lives. Hence the apostle James says, "Faith, if it hath not works, is dead." (James 2:17) Works are not a *prerequisite to* salvation, but they ought to be an *evidence of* salvation. Only God can respond to our faith; our fellow men respond to the overt behavior pattern which our faith has created. *Faith in action* is the substance of our glorifying God on Earth and perhaps attracting others to His divine plan. Faith is the vital substance which was lacking in the four decadent generations, allowing their arrogance and corruption to increase.

THE LION. The first great animal used in this quaternary is the lion, the king of the beasts, the strongest of animals. In the Hebrew, the word for "strongest" is *gibbor* which more nearly means mightiest, implying courage and ferocity as well as strength. Of course, lions do have great strength; a lion has been known to pick up a camel and throw him over a six-foot hedge. His courage will inspire him to attack almost any other animal, and his attack is notoriously fierce. So Solomon says, he "turneth not away for any." This is a beast which is beautiful in action, and exciting to watch.

A Christian's character should be analogous to this mighty lion's. It should be fearless. Do you know that fear is a mental attitude sin? It is a blasphemy against the character of God. Christ in his perfect veracity, immutability and omniscience, has exhorted believers to "fear not them who kill the body, but are not able to kill the soul; but rather fear him (God) who is able to destroy both soul and body in hell." (Matthew 10:28) We are to exhibit courage, and seek to please God and not man, expecially those of the decadent generations.

THE WAR-HORSE. What is called a "greyhound" in verse 21 is actually a war-horse in the Hebrew. A war horse was a special kind of horse, well-armored and well-trained for *battle*. In Ephesians 6:11-17, we note just what kind of specialized armor a Christian should possess: truth, righteousness, the gospel of peace, faith, salvation and the Word of God, i.e., Bible doctrine. Armored with this attitude and knowledge of Bible doctrine, a Christian should perform well in the battle of the faith. It should be noted that our enemies are much more dangerous than the enemies of the war horse. "We wrestle not against flesh and blood, but against principalities, against powers, against the rulers of the darkness of this world, against spiritual wickedness in high places." (Ephesians 6:12)

THE HE-GOAT. The next animal in this quaternary of great animals is the "he-goat," a ram, an extremely aggressive animal. A he-goat has been known to butt a locomotive head-on. Of course he came out second best in that encounter, but the point is that he, like the lion, is not afraid of anything. Many Christians in this tragic 20th Century are passive and reticent to engage the devil's domain. This reticence, sometimes called "separation," is not a symptom of faith. Timidity may well be a sympton of carnality; it may also be a symptom of an unsuccessful Christian life. Passivity and reticence are not characteristics of the he-goat, the ram. We must be "bold in the Lord," as were the Spirit-filled apostles, whose actions are described in the Book of Acts.

THE KING. The last illustration from verse 31 is "a king, against whom there is no rising up." This is not just any kind of king, but it is a king who rules effectively and justly. There is no insurrection, no rebellion, no revolution in the streets, for it is dealt with promptly, if severely.

A lack of rebellion can mean two things. First, there may be no revolution because there is no discontent. The country may be so well run that there is little if any reason for grievance. Secondly, if there is a minority of violent dissenters, a wrong crowd, they are dealt with peremptorily. Hence this "king" protects the rights of the majority of the people from the wrong crowd, and in so doing he creates the climate for maximum freedom, maximum dissemination of Bible doctrine. A king who can bring stability is a successful leader. Very likely Solomon had David in mind as a good example. Conversely we can view Solomon's son, Rehoboam as a prime exhibit of an unsuccessful leader, one who listened to the wrong crowd and ruined the nation.

In summary, we have eight characters to inspire us toward successful Christian living. They are the ant, the cony, the locust, the lizard, all small creatures, and the lion, the war-horse, the he-goat, and the ruling king, all great examples of faith in action. These contribute stability to a society or to a nation. Four generations led by these kind of people can establish an entire civilization. This kind of leadership and this kind of faith prevents social decadence. Paul's high standard of faith is again the example. "I can do *all* things through Christ which strengtheneth me." (Philippians 4:13)

How to Lose Friends and Alienate People

The last two verses of Chapter 30 illustrate some of the reasons for and consequences of ignoring Bible doctrine, exhibited in the preceding quaternaries.

If thou hast done foolishly in lifting up thyself,
Or if thou hast thought evil,
Lay thine hand upon thy mouth.
Surely the churning of milk bringeth forth butter,
And the wringing of the nose bringeth forth blood;
So the forcing of wrath bringeth forth strife.
Proverbs 30:32-33

The believer's greatest enemy as suggested in verse 32 is mental attitude sin, "evil" thoughts. This will neutralize one's testimony and stop the action of faith faster than anything else. One of the worst of mental attitude sins is pride, described as "foolishly lifting up thyself." Pride demonstrates stupidity. Whatever we may have accomplished is due to the grace of God in creating us and in preserving us. He could destroy all the details of life in a single instant.

Many other mental attitude sins are implied in the second line. Thinking evil could be anything from guilt reaction to hatred or jealousy. Proud people think they do not need doctrine. Evil thinkers reject doctrine because it convicts them, and leaves them uncomfortable. These sins, *even more* than the more obvious overt sins, destroy a Christian's faith and pervert his actions. Consequently the person who habitually practices such mental attitude sins is asked to keep his mouth shut. In other words, do not try to lead, do not try to witness if your life is not in harmony with the standards set forth in God's Word. Your character will only attract derision, and your actions will encourage only decadence. There will be no glorification of God.

In verse 33, there is another condition which demands that one stop talking. The verse begins by describing two cause-and-effect natural phenomena. If you churn milk, you get butter. If you wring a nose, you get blood. The fostering of anger produces strife. Anger leads to strife just as other mental attitude sins lead to various overt sins. An angry person cannot contain his wrath. He or she becomes a trouble-maker, already described in principle in one of the quaternaries. The apostle James has taught us that we are to be "slow to wrath, for the wrath of man worketh not the righteousness of God." (James 1:19-20) Anger exhibits a lack of self-discipline and a lack of grace orientation.

Fellow believers, like ourselves, will always be highly imperfect. The secret then is not to be occupied with people, since they will always fall short of our expectations. To be occupied with Christ should be our goal; His character fulfills and exceeds our highest hopes. Mental attitude sins are subtle and we all have them; they are difficult to avoid. But doctrine will teach us to recognize them, to understand them, and to Rebound* (I John 1:9). Then the Church will be full of ants, conies, locusts and lizards, and society will be led by lions, war-horses, he-goats and good kings.

CHAPTER VI

The Preservation of a Nation

Wisdom crieth without; she uttereth her voice in the streets.
She crieth in the chief place of concourse, in the openings of the gates:
In the city she uttereth her words, saying,

How long, ye simple ones, will ye love simplicity?
And the scorners delight in their scorning, and fools hate knowledge?
Turn you at my reproof: behold, I will pour out my spirit unto you,
I will make known my words unto you.

Because I have called, and ye refused;
I have stretched out my hand, and no man regarded;
But ye have set at nought all my counsel, and would none of my reproof:
I also will laugh at your calamity; I will mock when your fear cometh;
When your fear cometh as desolation, and your destruction cometh as a whirlwind; when distress and anguish cometh upon you.

Then shall they call upon me, but I will not answer;
They shall seek me early, but they shall not find me:
For that they hated knowledge, and did not choose the
    fear of the Lord:
They would none of my counsel: they despised all my
    reproof.
Therefore shall they eat of the fruit of their own way,
And be filled with their own devices.
For the turning away of the simple shall slay them,
And the prosperity of fools shall destroy them.

But whoso hearkeneth unto me shall dwell safely,
And shall be quiet from fear of evil.
Proverbs 1:20-33

Divine Institutions

"THE WORD OF GOD liveth and abideth forever." By these words, our Lord meant that the teachings and effects of God's Word cannot be abrogated. Its presence in the hearts and minds of mankind cannot be annihilated. Satan has devised innumerable strategies designed to remove the Word of God from the human race. But there has always been a remnant of people under God's protection who have preserved the Bible. This Bible contains *divine viewpoint* that never changes nor loses its relevance, although the world constantly changes.

One everlasting principle that is deduced from the Word of God is the principle of divine institutions. There are four of these institutions which are designed to protect the human race and to give it order and decency in carrying out its existence. The four divine institutions taught by Bible doctrine are as follows:

1. Individual Volition (free will)
2. Marriage
3. Family Life
4. National Entity

Each of the last three institutions are plural entities. It will be noted that Communism corrupts all four divine institutions. It denies the individual's right to determine his own life style; replaces freedom with slavery. It views marriage and family life as a mere convenience which is subject to the rule of the State. Its long

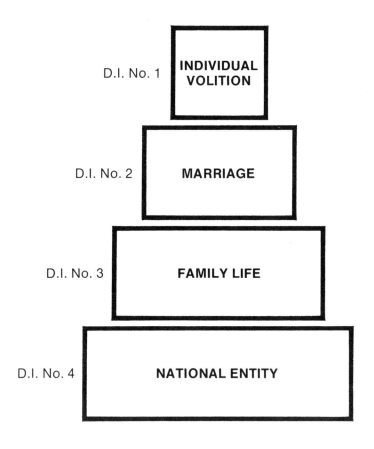

The Four Divine Institutions_____Figure **3**

range goal is the substitution of a single totalitarian and atheistic world government in place of the current plurality of national entities.

In this chapter, there will be an examination of the relationship between two of the divine institutions, Family Life and the National Entity. No nation can survive if the parents that comprise that nation do not live and teach Bible doctrine to their children. Since the family unit is designed to operate in a relaxed atmosphere, and since it is natural to learn from one's parents, the family unit is the *best* tool we have to communicate doctrine. The New Testament also teaches the value of the local church to be a place of family education in divine viewpoint and thus a perfect supplement to all Divine Institutions.

Too many people put their faith in America's past record of success or its external greatness, and ignore their personal responsibility in preparing their children to preserve, through military means if necessary, this great nation of ours. Freedom is not a self-perpetuating quantity. Since it is the condition under which a maximum number of people can be saved, Satan is naturally going to work extensively to destroy freedom wherever it exists. Therefore, it must be won anew by each successive generation.

America is presently the single greatest nation in the world by four standards of measurement: affluence, influence, economic power and military might. Today, America is beginning to decline in all four areas. However, more importantly, we are currently at the lowest point in our history in the area of knowledge of Bible doctrine. This means that America is in danger. Although our foreign policy may claim to be opposed to Communism, our domestic policies are becoming more and more socialistic.

Our public school systems have refused to acknowledge God (much less teach Bible doctrine). They have attempted to maintain a ragged kind of neutralist position, hoping to offend no one. However, there is no such thing in this world as a moral vacuum. The absence of good is the presence of evil.

Unfortunately, American Christianity has long been in a struggle between humanism and legalism, with political and theological pressure exercised by whichever side has predominated at any given time. Fundamentalists have been largely legalistic, and liberals have been mostly humanistic. So grace-oriented Christianity has seldom wielded any real influence.

In the past, dependent on the then-current nature of the Church, Christianity has been alternately endorsed, hated, honored, ridiculed or subverted. Nevertheless, Bible doctrine has provided the root of righteousness in this country, and without it, America has no place to go but down. Our philosophy of nationalism and economics has supported the greatest amount of freedom and success that the world has ever known, and it comes from the principles inherent in the Word of God. But now, Bible doctrine is derided for being 'irrelevant to the needs of the modern world.'

We believe that the solution for the preservation of any Christian nation is in the succeeding generation. Bible doctrine must be passed along from parents to children if the next generation is to continue to enjoy the blessings of the past, for blessings are not distributed arbitrarily. They are the result of learning and living divine viewpoint. How is this continuity to be attained? The Book of Deuteronomy is directed to teaching the citizens of the Israelite commonwealth how to live as a nation. Let us observe in Deuteronomy for a moment to see how the Jews were instructed to pass their knowledge of God from one generation to the next. The secret of their success, despite many adverse circumstances, is to be found in Deuteronomy 6:5-9:

> *And thou shalt love the Lord thy God with all thine heart.*
> *And with all thy soul, and with all thy might.*
> *And these words, which I command thee this day, shall*
>   *be in thine heart.*
> *And thou shalt teach them diligently unto thy children.*
> *And shalt talk of them when thou sittest in thine house,*
> *And when thou walkest by the way,*
> *And when thou liest down, and when thou risest up.*
> *And thou shalt bind them for a sign upon thine hand,*
> *And they shall be as frontlets between thine eyes.*
> *And thou shalt write them upon the posts of thy house,*
>   *and on thy gates.*

When parents sit down with their children, they talk Bible doctrine; when they go out walking they talk doctrine; when they go to bed at night and when they get up in the morning they talk doctrine. In other words, they are to surround their children with so much doctrine in the course of ordinary family activities that those children cannot help but learn it. This is not a simple matter of quoting scriptures. Anyone can quote scripture, but it means nothing unless the meaning behind it is taught and applied. The current anti-spiritual trend in America today could be reversed if we could equip enough teenagers with Bible doctrine.

What would be a worthwhile reformation or revival? Spiritual renewal with permanent impact results in Bible study going on in church and, consequently, in the homes. Revival lasts only as long as there is emphasis on the Word of God. Revival does not have to directly involve a majority of the population. A small minority of people can preserve a nation if that small minority of people are really living doctrine.

For example, the Assyrian Empire was in serious decline when Jonah was sent by God to Ninevah (in 756 B.C.) where he preached the gospel so dynamically that the city was converted. New principles were established, and perhaps new leadership as well. For the next one hundred years Assyria remained a world power, although she had been teetering on the brink of disaster before Jonah's arrival.

Later, the Chaldean state was a small collection of remnant peoples from the Assyrian Empire when Nebuchadnezzar was converted. He put the prophet Daniel in a position of authority and leadership to spread Bible doctrine over his domain. With policies based on Bible doctrine, the Chaldean Empire continued to grow in power and wealth. Later it disintegrated under Nebuchadnezzar's grandson, Belshazzar, an unregenerate drunkard, a human monster (539 B.C.).

For a more modern example, one might look at Great Britain which became great in the wake of the Puritans, who established Bible doctrine. On several occasions, England was in decline or facing disaster when revival came and the land was restored. The Puritan, Presbyterian, Quaker and Methodist revivals resulted in the founding of churches all over the land and the world. It has been said that during Puritan times, when one strolled by the open windows of a village home, one could often hear parents reading the Bible to their children, not only at the evening meal but throughout the day. Those children were the salvation of England for generations to come. They were a sturdy lot. Given this background and a Biblical world view, England colonized three continents, and its missionaries brought the Gospel of Christ and Bible doctrine to millions of Africans, Chinese and Indians. All this was possible because as a national entity, they had wisdom from the Word of God. Later, in the 19th century, England embraced evolution and Fabian socialism. On the basis of our own knowledge of doctrine[1], we could easily predict that 100 years later she would be a fourth rate power with little heritage and little influence.

The Five Cycles of Discipline

What are the consequences of a nation's ignoring Bible doctrine? God has a special way of dealing with any nation called by His name, be it Israel (a Hebrew commonwealth) or a Christian commonwealth such as England or the United States of America. Many blessings are promised to the nation which follows the Lord; and, conversely, five cycles of discipline are promised to a nation which rejects Bible doctrine. We shall first consider the five cycles of discipline. They apply historically to the Jewish nation; and they also apply to any Christian commonwealth. Just as a parent only disciplines his own children, so God's disciplines do not apply to pagan nations or empires such as Imperial Rome, the Mogul Empire or Soviet Russia for the obvious reason that these entities have no Biblical base for national life.

When a national entity, and particularly the leaders thereof, reject Bible doctrine, the Love of God is stifled. His character, like that of a concerned parent, requires that discipline be administered. The judgment of God follows an overlapping, not a clear-cut sequential pattern. It comes in five stages, each successively more severe. The five visitations of God's disciplines upon Israel, as prophesied by Moses, are found in Leviticus 26:14-46. While the disciplines that Moses specifically describes are a warning to Israel in particular, the same disciplines, in general, are also applied to Christian nations who repeatedly reject Bible doctrine and walk in disharmony with God's plan. It is discipline designed for national entities who "will not hearken unto me, and will not do all these commandments." (Leviticus 26:14)

While the details of each cycle of discipline will vary from one era to another, the general principle behind each cycle remains.

---

[1]Such as the four decadent generations, the four social parasites, Chapter V.

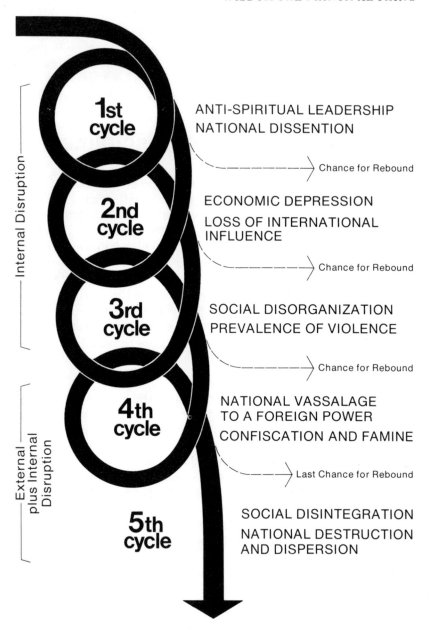

The Five Cycles
of National Discipline———————————Figure **4**

This principle is to cause the inhabitants to repent of their disobedience.

Cycle I: Anti-Spiritual Leadership and National Dissention

The first cycle of discipline begins under leaders who no longer care about the people. The high principles on which the nation was founded have become perverted. The rulers are now primarily concerned with gaining personal power and wealth rather than protecting the welfare of their subjects. The *old sin nature** rules in the lives of the national leaders, and hence the principle of leadership in its highest form is severely distorted. When this condition becomes prevalent God will send His first discipline, holding back His full anger in an attempt to cause the people to *Rebound*. His long-suffering character is displayed here.

> *And if ye shall despise my statutes, or if your soul abhor mine judgments, so that ye will not do all my commandments, but that ye break my covenent; I also will do this unto you: I will even appoint over you terror, consumption, and the burning ague, that shall consume the eyes and cause sorrow of heart; and ye shall sow your seed in vain, for your enemies shall eat it. And I will set my face against you, and ye shall be slain before your enemies; they that hate you shall reign over you, and ye shall flee when none pursueth you.*
> *Leviticus 26:14-17*

There will be a general loss of mental stability and, consequently, a loss of physical health. The people will lose the courage and the initiative that caused them to prosper and succeed in earlier generations. Instead they will become fearful and filled with terror, "Ye shall flee when none pursueth you." There will be fear concerning the enemies' supposed might and a desire to capitulate rather than defend the land. This first cycle will also experience a halt or a reversal from a dynamic economy to a stagnant one, "Ye shall sow your seed in vain." When all these things come upon a nation, they should, if they have been taught a sufficient amount of doctrine, realize that God is displeased with them, and that their wisest course is *repentance** and *rebound.** This will forestall the subsequent cycles of discipline, and restore a favorable national destiny. Unfortunately, the voices of men espousing Bible doctrine (prophets, preachers, etc.) that would warn the nation of increasing judgment are often silenced, sometimes by violent death, or at best heard but mocked and ignored. If such is the case, God (as a parent to a child) has no choice but to inflict the next cycle of His discipline.

Cycle II: Economic Depression and Loss of International Influence

The second cycle of discipline is, generally speaking, an increase in the intensity of the first cycle. Economic recession gives way to economic depression. The anti-spiritual leadership within the nation causes it to lose international influence. A first rate power begins to decline into a second rate power.

> *And if ye will not yet for all this hearken unto me, then I will punish you seven times more for your sins. And I will break the pride of your power; and I will make your heaven as iron, and your earth as brass, and your strength shall be spent in vain; for your land shall not yield her increase, neither shall the trees of the land yield their fruits.*
> *Leviticus 26:18-20*

The Bible uses language which abounds in agricultural, climatological, and military terms. They are not specifically applicable to industrial societies; yet the underlying principles still apply. In the First Cycle of Discipline, economic recession was described as a seed which was sown and apparently harvested, but not enjoyed. In Cycle 2, the seed does not ripen, suggestive of an increasingly severe economic crisis, depression rather than recession. Drought and want are pictured, "And I will break the pride of your power." This suggests that military victories are a thing of the past, and the current trend is toward military defeat. This is another indication of a leadership lacking in both courage and inspiration.

Cycle III: Social Disorganization and the Prevalence of Violence

If the previous two cycles of discipline are not sufficient to cause a nation to rebound, God must resort to His third cycle of discipline. (It must be borne in mind that each of these cycles overlap, but as the nation's decadence intensifies, so does its discipline.)

And if ye walk contrary unto me, and will not hearken unto me, I will bring seven times more plagues upon you according to your sins. I will also send wild beasts among you, which shall rob you of your children, and destroy your cattle, and make you few in number and your highways shall be desolate.
Leviticus 26:21-22

The prime characteristic of the third cycle is violence, here made analogous to "wild beasts." Undisciplined, disrespectful children mature into monsters, and monsters are now predominant in the population. These violent men will destroy the achievements of civilization. The streets become unsafe for travel. Crime rates will soar, and people will cease to dwell safely in their homes as the violence renders the populace "few in numbers." Some emigration may occur as sensible people become increasingly dissatisfied. This only adds to the general weakness and instability in the nation. For example, evidence America's cities disintegrating as the citizens rush into the suburbs, leaving the urban areas to decline into pockets of crime and immorality. As in finance, where poor economic policies discourage good businessmen from investing money, so poor leadership discourages good citizens from participating in government.

In recalling the doctrine taught in a previous chapter, "The Enticement of the Wrong Crowd," we realize that these beasts are not some supernatural visitation, but the natural product of a nation which ignores teaching Bible doctrine to its young people. The first characteristic of the wrong crowd that David describes is violence; they want to "lay wait for blood . . . lurk privily for the innocent without cause." (Proverbs 1:11)

God knows people and their old sin natures much better than they understand themselves; He knows that there are certain principles of human behavior that are as inevitable as the laws of nature. If one adds soda to vinegar, a chemical reaction is always expected in which the mixture bubbles off carbon dioxide. Similarly in the case of society, if a nation fails to add doctrine to the human soul, the old sin nature will develop unchecked and unrestrained. One product of the old sin nature is violence. In other words, society brings disaster upon itself (often a generation or so later) by rejecting Bible doctrine and by unleashing the old sin nature. God hardly needs to create some supernatural monsters to send among us; we create our own weird monsters. And the next generation pays the price.

Thus far, military reverses, political reverses, moral declines, social disorganizations and anti-spiritual leadership have been the prominent features of the first three cycles of national discipline. These are all internal troubles. With cycles 4 and 5, and an intensifying of the disciplines, external powers are brought into the land to occupy and subjugate the inhabitants. Liberty is suddenly restricted. Taxation becomes brutal. The anti-spiritual leadership loses its popularity, and old times are relished; reminiscences of better days encourage rebound as the nation looks for new leadership. Thus from Cycle 3 to Cycle 4, the dimension of discipline changes.

Cycle IV: National Vassalage and Internal Famine

The Fourth Cycle of Discipline is a natural result of the breakdown of society as is experienced in the third cycle. Leadership is poor, the economy is stagnant, the society is terrorized, the morale is low, the motivation to defend the land is gone. One example of the fourth cycle of discipline on Judah is its vassalage to Babylon, a national humiliation. Judah was owned by Nebuchadnezzar. Another example is their vassalage to Imperial Rome during the New Testament times. The nation was at the mercy of alien kings and emperors.

> *And I will bring a sword upon you, that shall avenge the quarrel of my covenant; and when ye are gathered together within your cities, I will send the pestilence among you; and ye shall be delivered into the hand of the enemy. And when I have broken the staff of your bread, ten women shall bake your bread in one oven, and they shall deliver you your bread again by weight: and ye shall eat, and not be satisfied.*
> *Leviticus 26:25-26*

The two leading characteristics of this cycle are (1) military collapse and (2) breadlines. "Ye shall eat, and not be satisfied;" all sense of contentment is lost. Worse, however, is military invasion and occupation. This implies that the decline of the nation is well along. God uses other nations as His "whips." Historical examples of this would be the Egyptian, Assyrian, Babylonian and Roman subjugations of Israel. Other nations used to "whip" Israel in the days of the Judges were the Midianites, the Moabites, the Ammonites and the Philistines.

In Biblical history, more often than not, Israel rebounded under the imposition of the Fourth Cycle of Discipline. New leadership, which had long been needed was now sought. Such men as Gideon, Jephthah, Isaiah, and the Maccabees are now listened to, and eagerly followed. Bible doctrine becomes increasingly considered as trials deepen. As individuals return to Bible doctrine, and heed spiritual leadership, the basis for national deliverance is laid. Sometimes Israel rebounded at this stage of discipline (particularly during the days of the Judges). But sometimes Israel did not rebound at this critical juncture, thus ushering in the Fifth Cycle, the culmination of the previous four.

Cycle V: National Destruction

Israel was in Palestine from approximately 1410 B.C. to 135 A.D., a period of about 1500 years. During these fifteen centuries, they experienced the Fourth Cycle of Discipline about nine times. Six of the nine times, they recognized new leadership such as the judges or prophets, and became dissatisfied with the fruits of apostasy. Men such as Gideon, Isaiah and Judas Maccabeus arose to re-establish divine viewpoint and freedom. The people rebounded and a measure of freedom and prosperity were restored.

But three times, Israel in the Fourth Cycle did not rebound. They entered into the terrible Fifth Cycle, an unforgettable and regrettable experience. Once was in 721 B.C. when the Northern Kingdom refused the counsel of prophets such as Amos, Jonah and Hosea. Assyrians sacked Israel's capital city, Samaria, and the Jews were led in captivity, or slavery from the land. A second time was in 586 B.C. when the Southern Kingdom of Judah refused the counsel of Baruch, Ezekiel, Jeremiah and others. Chaldeans sacked Jerusalem, destroyed the temple, drove the populace into slavery, and levelled the city.

The third time was the climax of another apostasy and rebellion, this time against Rome. The prophets they spurned (and burned, beheaded, stoned, imprisoned, etc.) included John the Baptist, Stephen, James the Lord's brother, Paul, John and many others. Christ the Redeemer was unwelcome, and was crucified. The new group of protesters, the Christian Church of Jerusalem, was hounded and persecuted into migration. Before Christ's crucifixion He stated several times that the Fifth Cycle was but one generation away, but forty years, and it was. The Fifth Cycle has at least five characteristics.

1. Cannibalism and Famine

And ye shall eat the flesh of your sons and the flesh of your daughters shall ye eat.
Leviticus 26:29

During the siege of 587-586 B.C., Jerusalem was surrounded for 18 months by Babylonian armies; famine staked the populace; cannibalism was reported. During the siege of 68-70 A.D., Jerusalem was surrounded by Roman armies for three years. Factions within the city fought each other, assassinated rival leaders, and even burned each other's grain. The food supplies completely gave out, and once again cannibalism was reported, this time by Josephus.

2. Destruction of the City and the Temple

And I will destroy your high places, and cut down your images, and cast your carcasses of your idols, and my soul shall abhor you. And I will make your cities waste, and bring your sanctuaries unto desolation. Leviticus 26:30-31
Leviticus 26:30-31

Jerusalem was levelled in 586 B.C., including Solomon's Temple, one of the Seven Wonders of the Ancient World. Similarly in 70 A.D., Herod's Temple was destroyed. Later, in 135 A.D., the entire city was plowed under, so that yet another rebellion would have no city for a focal point. Josephus has suggested that 1,100,000 people perished in this second siege, in 70 A.D., some by disease, some by starvation, some by cannibalism and some by

Roman arms.[2] Another 500,000 are estimated to have died in the destruction of 135 A.D.

3. Ravaged Countryside

And I will bring the land into desolation: and your enemies which dwell therein shall be astonished at it.
Leviticus 26:32

A city can be destroyed and fairly rapidly rebuilt, if the countryside is left intact, and its economic base remains undisturbed. Jerusalem was so thoroughly destroyed in 586 B.C. that the general region became uninhabited. In 70 A.D., the Romans after destroying the city, allowed it to be rebuilt. Sixty-five years later, they found they faced another rebellion, again centering around Jerusalem and the Jews perverted concept of a military destiny. The city was plowed under and Jews were eliminated from the land for good. Significant Jewish resettlement of Palestine did not then recur until this present century, some 1800 years later.

4. Geographical Dispersion

And I will scatter you among the heathen, and will draw out a sword after you: . . . And ye shall perish among the heathen, and the land of your enemies shall eat you up.
Leviticus 26:33, 38

An era of spiritual, moral, judicial and economic declension occurred just before the Fifth Cycle in 586 B.C. The leaders of Jerusalem rejected Biblical ethics (as so lucidly presented in the Proverbs) and they rejected the concept of a spiritual destiny for the nation, preferring an imperial, military destiny. Similarly in the era just preceding the Fifth Cycle in 70 A.D., the leaders of Jerusalem chose terrorism over peace; the zealots, who chose militarism rather than a spiritual destiny, persecuted the early church. They chose apostasy* rather than redemption through the crucifixion of our Lord; they also rejected Biblical ethics, both in the form of Solomon's Proverbs and Christ's parables and Sermon on the Mount.

---

[2]Flavius Josephus, *Three Books of The Jewish War*, Vol. VI, trans. William Whiston, Bridgeport: Published by M. Sherman, 1828, Book V, ch. IX, pp. 42-43.

The developments which occurred within the ill-fated Jerusalem in the era from 60 to 70 A.D. are recorded by the historian Josephus, and they make one wonder how depraved, distorted and uncompassionate leadership can get. Josephus, who was an eye-witness, could hardly believe the events perpetrated within the doomed city.

Following the desolation of the Holy City, both in 586 B.C. and in 70 A.D., a forced exodus and enslavement of Jews took place. Hundreds of thousands of Jewish survivors in Palestine became Roman slaves, manned the galleys, or were served to the lions in the Coliseum. This is called the "dispersion" or the "Diaspora." The 586 B.C. dispersion lasted 70 years, after which Jerusalem and Judah were resettled, and God's people, spiritually renewed, proceeded along lines established by Bible doctrine. The second dispersion, which began in 70 A.D., will not end until the Second Advent*, at which time the Jews will repent of their rejection of the Messiah and turn to Him for deliverance.

5. Spirit of Dejection and Fear

And upon them that are left alive of you I will send a faintness into their hearts in the lands of their enemies; and the sound of a shaken leaf shall chase them; and they shall flee, as fleeing from a sword; and they shall flee when none pursueth. And they that are left of you shall pine away in their iniquity in your enemies' lands; and also in the iniquities of their father shall they pine away with them.
Leviticus 26:36-39

Proverbs teaches courage, an attribute associated with spiritual strength.[3] This warning reflects a lack of courage, and a continuing lack of rebound. Proverbs teaches an Edification Complex* which results in social harmony; this too is lacking in Cycle 5, with self-pity predominating in its stead. Leviticus paints a picture of perpetual sorrow whereas Proverbs teaches harmony with God, and repeats the doctrine of the "merry heart." Here again in the Fifth Cycle is a symptom of a negative volition* and its logical re-

---

[3]See Chapter V, "The Wisdom of Agur," Quaternary F.

sults, crying and pining in their iniquity rather than rebounding in God's grace.

Once again, it is to be observed that the Five Cycles of Discipline increase in intensity. They tend to overlap in their development and envelopment, like successive cycles of a coil. This is to suggest that it is not as if one cycle was completed before the second cycle began, as links in a chain would illustrate. It is to be observed that the first three cycles are exclusively internal, whereas Cycles Four and Five include subjugation by an alien national power.

One of God's characteristics is longsuffering. It requires three to five successive generations of failure to usher in the Fifth Cycle. Another characteristic of God is dependability; if He threatens discipline, He will deliver it.

In the Church Age, Christian-influenced nations are responsible to advance holy principles and protect the freedom of their citizens. When leadership becomes anti-spiritual, when recessions develop into depressions, when international influence declines, when internal social disorganization becomes rife, and when national weakness leads to destructive wars, many of the conditions calling for divine wrath are developing. Even as a parent disciplines a child, the severity depending on the nature of the infraction, so when nations feel the brunt of divine discipline, it should be considered as correction by a loving parent, which Proverbs discusses at some length.

The Cry of Wisdom

Wisdom crieth without;
She uttereth her voice in the streets,
She crieth in the chief place of concourse, in the openings
of the gates,
In the city she uttereth her words, saying,
How long, ye simple ones, will ye love simplicity?
And the scorners delight in their scorning, and fools
hate knowledge?
Proverbs 1:20-22

Wisdom 'crying- without' is a reference to a speaker giving out information, and it could well be a prophet such as Jeremiah, Paul or Christ warning Israel of the Fifth Cycle of Discipline. God gives a nation time to repent by sending preliminary warnings in the form of lesser disciplines, as has just been observed. In later centuries, Isaiah, Hosea, Amos, Jeremiah, and John the Baptist repeatedly warned Israel to repent and turn back to God. Proverbs anticipated those times. "She" in verses 20 and 21 is "wisdom," and "she" is trying to reach the people from every possible vantage point. "The chief place of concourse" is an open air amphitheater; the "openings of the gates" is a platform above every city gate where men stood to give the daily news. The informed and concerned Jews were trying every means of ancient communication available to them to reach the people, to expose the nation to as much doctrine as possible.

What does wisdom say? "How long, ye simple ones, will ye love simplicity?" The Hebrew word for "simple ones" is the word *pethim*, and this sentence might be more literally translated as, 'how long, ye stupid ones, will ye love stupidity?' A stupid Christian is a Christian who has no knowledge of doctrine in his mind. Since his brain has to be active, and since he has no doctrine to control his thoughts, a vacuum is created into which may come mental attitude sins and occupations with the details of life.

On a national scale, this would be called licentiousness and materialism. This is not to say that our material blessings are sinful, but simply that we should not allow ourselves to look to them for happiness or security. They are peripheral and not central. As Hebrews 13:5 says, "Let your conversation (manner of life) be without covetousness, and be content with such things as ye have; for he hath said, I will never leave thee, nor forsake thee."

Any Christian who is stupid and does not apply the above doctrine has double misery. Misery No. 1 comes in this life when his details fail, and he loses happiness and joy. Misery No. 2 comes after he dies. He will go to Heaven, but will find that there is no reward for anyone who lived for temporal and selfish goals (treasures that are laid up on Earth).

Wisdom addresses herself to three categories of people. The first category includes the 'stupid ones' who have just been described; they are indeed indifferent. They are not particularly antagonistic towards doctrine, they just do not care about it. The second category is the "scorner." He actively opposes Bible doctrine by ridiculing it or criticizing it. The third category is the hater and Proverbs 1:22 called him a "fool." He hates doctrine because it is teaching that convicts him of his guilt.

These three categories include both the saved and the unsaved. Simple (stupid) unbelievers are those who are indifferent to their need to be reconciled to God through acceptance of His grace in the person of Jesus Christ. Indifferent believers ignore their need for learning Christian Life Techniques once they are past the point of propitiation, or salvation. The scorning Christian thinks there is something more important than Bible doctrine. He supposes he can please God by being emotional or by doing human works. He lives by human viewpoint rather than by divine viewpoint. The scornful unbeliever does not think he needs God's grace. The haters, both Christian and non-Christian, are offended by the teaching of Bible doctrine because it reveals their sinfulness. When indifferent, scornful and foolish Christians predominate, the Church is in great danger. Paul warned Timothy that such activity would be a prelude to the last days.

> *For the time will come when they will not endure sound doctrine but, after their own lusts, shall they heap to themselves teachers, having itching ears; and they shall turn away their ears from the truth.*
> *II Timothy 4:3-4*

Just as the Bible is the foundation for the Church, Christians are the foundation of a nation. When the foundation of a nation collapses, the nation will go down too. In the Book of Matthew, Christ spoke of believers as the "salt of the earth,"

> *Ye are the salt of the earth, but if the salt have lost its savor, with what shall it be salted: It is thereafter good for nothing, but to be cast out, and to be trodden under foot of men.*
> *Matthew 5:13*

When he spoke these words, Christ had in mind the Old Testament use of salt as a preservative in meat. Christians act as a preservative in a nation. What we do makes the difference between a completely evil world and a restrained evil world. If we successfully fulfill our preservative purpose, what will be the result?

> *Turn you at my reproof; behold, I will pour out my spirit unto you, I will make known my words unto you.*
> *Proverbs 1:23*

"Turn" is the Hebrew word *shub*. This means to turn around, 180°, but there are two facets to its meaning. The first step is repentance or rebound *from* sin. The second step is turning *toward* Bible doctrine to fill in the gap. The "you" He speaks to is the believer; it only takes a small but sincere minority of believers to affect an entire nation.

There are two things that follow repentance. The first, as seen in line 2, is the filling of the spirit*. The second gift of God is knowledge, "my words." The combination of these two things will save a nation because righteousness will be exalted. We can express this principle in a mathematical formula that makes it easier to remember. FS + KD = DG, which translated means, "the filling of the spirit plus knowledge of doctrine equals divine good."

God has decreed that a Christian who is oriented can affect the lives of a large number of fellow citizens. However, the adverse is also true. If a Christian does not have Bible doctrine, the line of blessing is cut off from Christian to non-Christian, and the nation suffers on a mass scale.

A nation which is truly oriented to the divine plan always produces two things: internal strength (which we will call spiritual muscle) and external strength (in the form of military power). This is not to say that Christians should trust in armaments, but military muscle is what an unregenerate enemy recognizes. Nationalism is endorsed by the Word of God. We have the right, and in fact the obligation, to fight for the preservation of our nation. In Romans 13:1-7, Paul describes the Christian's responsibility to support his nation; in sum he says, "the powers that be are ordained of God. Whosoever, therefore, resisteth the power, resisteth the ordinance of God; and they that resist shall receive to themselves damnation." History has shown that when a nation loses its spiritual muscle, it inevitably loses its military muscle as well. There is, conversely, no such thing as military defeat for a nation that has spiritual muscle.

Some may find it difficult to believe that America's complex problems could be solved by Bible doctrine. But few people realize the wide applications of Bible doctrine. Doctrine can be used effectively to determine foreign policy and, in particular, military policy. Many, with some justice, refer to ours as a "post-Christian nation." Most people, lacking Bible doctrine, ignore the application of Christian principles to areas of national security. They should be chided just as sternly as Isaiah chided Hezekiah, who graciously but foolishly received the Babylonian ambassadors in the 7th Century B.C., circa 690 B.C. (Isaiah 39)

When Isaiah asked Hezekiah, "What have they seen in thine house?", all Hezekiah could answer was, "My treasures." Hezekiah had told the heathen ambassadors nothing of the sovereign Lord of Hosts, Maker of Heaven and Earth, Creator of Life, who had only recently delivered the Israelites from national disaster during the Assyrian invasion. Thus, Hezekiah inspired envy rather than fear or respect in the minds of the Babylonian State Department. They would return to their homeland to report, and later, to plot a campaign against Jerusalem to acquire the gold which Hezekiah had so naively displayed. Material wealth inspires envy and jealousy in one's neighbors, whereas, spirituality inspires respect and fear. Our State Department might do better to display our wealth less, and our spiritual heritage more.

Isaiah's words may well be applied to us, just as much as to Hezekiah, when he said,

> *"Behold the days come, that all that is in thine house, and that which thy fathers have laid up in store until this day, shall be carried to Babylon; nothing shall be left, saith the Lord."*
> *Isaiah 39:6*

When individual Christians fail to do the Will of God, they are disciplined. When Christians collectively fail to do God's will, their nation is punished. Judah's sister nation, Israel (or Ephraim, the ten northern tribes), also failed God miserably. Hosea addressed the following words to Ephraim:

> *Therefore shalt thou fall in the day, and the prophet also shalt fall with thee in the night, and I will destroy thy mother. My people are destroyed for lack of knowledge; I will also reject thee, that thou shalt be no priest to me; seeing thou hast forgotten the law of thy God, I will also forget thy children. As they were increased, so they sinned against me; therefore will I change their glory into shame.*
> *Hosea 4:5-7*

The first line here indicates that disaster will fall suddenly, and at that time there will be no way out. This is national disaster in the form of military defeat and captivity. The leaders of Ephraim (Northern Israel) were given over to the old sin nature. Drunkenness, idolatry and immorality of all kinds were prevalent in the land. All this is described earlier in the same chapter,

> *By swearing, and lying, and killing, and stealing, and*
> *committing adultery they break out, and blood touchest*
> *blood.*
> *Hosea 4:2*

The word "swearing" refers to dishonest business practices. This, accompanied by lying, murder, theft, adultery and violence, paints a picture of a nation in the lowest levels of depravity. But does it not sound very similar to our own situation? At this time, Ephraim was even involved in a very sloppy form of socialism, and since the country was full of parasites, the economy was gradually being drained. These northern tribes had little indigenous military strength of their own, so they frequently went south to Judah for help. However, they could not depend on an ally forever. After giving Ephraim three generations of warning, God allowed them to be taken into captivity by the Assyrians under Sargon II.

Hosea, a prophet in the northern kingdom, was warning them, because the Holy Spirit had given him information about what was going to happen and why. In verse 5, he uses the term, "thy mother," which is an idiom for the structure of a society within a national entity. He means then that Ephraim's entire cultural heritage was going to be destroyed. The people were going to be dispersed and sent into slavery. Why? Verse 6 gives us the answer, "for lack of knowledge." One thing that a nation cannot do without is knowledge of divine viewpoint.

The result is that "thou shalt be no priest to me." In other words, since they were ignoring doctrine, the nation could no longer function as the intermediary between God and the rest of the human race. The next result was that, "I will also forget thy children." The next generation was going to be taken into captivity. The "glory" that Israel had had, materially speaking, was going to be turned into "shame;" she was going to lose her economic prosperity. All this began because Ephraim had lost her spiritual muscle. A later chapter in Hosea shows the Lord's reaction to the fall of His chosen people,

> *O Ephraim, what shall I do unto thee? O Judah, what shall*
> *I do unto thee? For your goodness is like a morning*

cloud, and like the early dew it goeth away. Therefore
have I hewed them by the prophets; I have slain them by
the words of my mouth; and thy judgments are as the
light that goeth forth. For I desired mercy, and not sacri-
fice, and the knowledge of God more than burnt offerings.
Hosea 6:4-6

The judgments of God are compared to the swiftness of light,
which travels 186,000 miles per second. They come so quickly
that there is no escape. The Lord desires knowledgeable worship
and not mere ritual, e.g., "burnt offerings."

Now our attention will return to Proverbs. David is dealing
with the same things that are at issue in the Books of Hosea and
Isaiah, the turning away of a nation from Bible doctrine.

Because I have called, and ye refused:
I have stretched out my hand, and no man regardeth,
But ye have set at naught all my counsel,
And would have none of my reproof,
I will also laugh at your calamity;
I will mock when your fear cometh;
When your fear cometh as desolation,
And your destruction cometh as a whirlwind;
When distress and anguish come upon you.
Proverbs 1:24-27

God has always given mankind a maximum amount of time to
repent, and He tries every means He has to reach man's volition.
Finally, if after all His efforts, a nation still refuses to recognize
its need for repentance, God is left no recourse but to exercise His
wrath and laugh at the foolishness of mankind. This is not a sadis-
tic laughter, but one that comes after maximum effort that has
failed; it is the only alternative to tears. Again in verse 27, there is
a reference to the swiftness of God's judgment, "as a whirlwind."

What happens after a disaster? Do the people who refused to
heed doctrine before the disaster suddenly become strong and
heroic? Unfortunately not!

Then shall they call upon me, but I will not answer;
They shall seek me early, but they shall not find me;
For they that hated knowledge
And did not choose the fear of the Lord.
They would have none of my counsel;

They despised all my reproof.
Therefore shall they eat of the fruit of their own way,
And be filled with their own devices.
For the turning away of the simple shall slay them,
And the prosperity of fools shall destroy them.
Proverbs 1:28-32

When disaster is imminent, when fear and confusion reign, then "They shall call upon me," the "me" in this case being "wisdom."

But people cannot absorb much Bible doctrine when they are under pressure. People can only learn in a relaxed atmosphere, before disaster strikes. So wisdom says, "I will not answer . . . they shall not find me." They will only be frightened and "up tight." They did not bother to learn the Doctrine of Faith-Rest, so they do not know how to respond in times of crisis. They have been occupied with the details of life, so when they are taken into captivity with only the clothes on their backs, they will panic to see their possessions going up in smoke or hauled off by their captors. The only thing that can come out of their minds at that time will be poor decisions. They cannot think of anything but survival, because when times were good they had no time for doctrine. When verse 30 says, "they would none of my counsel," it means they had no desire to learn doctrine. "They despised all my reproof" points out that they only became angry when the scriptures convicted them. Therefore, says verse 31, they will reap what they sowed.

The "turning away" in verse 32 is apostasy; stupid people apostasize and their apostasy destroys them. They turn from doctrine to details, described in the second line as "prosperity." They look to prosperity for security. They desire security more than pleasing God. How like contemporary America! When we turn from doctrine, the only thing left is human viewpoint. One of the prime areas where the folly of human viewpoint can be observed is in our foreign policy. Human viewpoint says, "Disarm and our enemies will see that we want peace, and they will not want to fight us." Anyone who is willing to face facts knows how foolish this is. The only things that makes an enemy unwilling to fight is the fear that he might lose.

The advocates of disarmament argue that a large force of arms only makes other people anxious to fight us. On the contrary, the primary purpose of such military means as atomic weaponry is to act as a deterrent. The more strength we have, the less our enemies want to risk death by fighting us. That is why political and military scientists with some knowledge of Bible doctrine say that it is foolish to state that we will never, under any circumstances, use our atomic weaponry. Once we have made a statement like that, the main advantage of atomic weapons is lost.

General Nathan Twining has written a book entitled *Neither Liberty Nor Safety*.[4] In this book, he discusses the foolishness of the men who opt for disarmament. He describes seven categories of people who are leading us toward destruction by their concept of limited warfare. They are listed as follows:

1. The scientist with a guilt complex
2. Low level State Department officials
3. Moralists
4. Political scientists of humanistic inclination
5. Defeatists
6. Unilateral disarmament believers
7. Military 'softies'

The *scientist with a guilt complex* is frightened by the damage done by nuclear weapons, and he feels a personal responsibility. He usually fails to see that in the one case where atomic weapons were used (Hiroshima and Nagasaki in 1945) the number of lives lost on those two days was much smaller than the number of either American or Japanese lives which would have been lost ultimately through conventional warfare.

The second category is the *low level State Department official*. Often these men are educated in humanistic viewpoint rather than divine viewpoint. They are living comfortably. They can adjust with surprising rapidity to new situations. They suggest "better red than dead."

The third category is the *moralists*. They are often pacifistic clergymen, who misapply the command, "Thou shalt not *murder*" to national defense. They forget that liberty has been purchased with blood several times. They are unaware of the tyranny of the old sin nature. They are "simple." (Proverbs 1:32)

Closely related to this last category are the *political scientists*

---

[4]Nathan F. Twining, *Neither Liberty Nor Safety: A Hard Look at U.S. Military Policy and Strategy*, New York: Holt, Rinehart & Winston, 1966.

on human viewpoint. They put their faith in their own theories, and the "goodwill" occasionally displayed by the enemy, to whom occasional goodwill is merely a part of the tactics of assault. They do not understand the climax of history as taught by the prophets, nor do they understand God's overlordship of history. They drift in the morass of finite humanism.

The fifth category General Twining discusses are the *defeatists* who think that nobody can win a nuclear war. The defeatist considers it progressive to disarm and reassure our nation's enemies that they will never have to fear atomic weaponry; meanwhile those enemies are busy building a superior defense and offense, including nuclear weapons. He forgets that (1) our first line of defense is our faith, and (2) our second is our weapons.

The sixth category is the *unilateral disarmament crowd.* They too are thinking with human viewpoint, and are subject to producing abominable advice. They have much in common with the moralists, the defeatists, the pacifists and others forgetful of what made this country truly great. Included among this group are the National Council of Churches spokesmen, who have woefully misapplied Biblical teachings.

The last category is found within the ranks of *the military itself,* a minority of soldiers who are influenced by the former six and have no real right to call themselves military men. All of the above categories of people profess the desire for national security, but they reject the basis for it: righteousness on the inside and strength on the outside. They are not courageous nor are they wise. They are vacillating and simple.

General Twining drew the title of his book from a statement by Benjamin Franklin that eloquently summarizes both his feelings and ours, "They that can give up essential liberty to obtain a little temporary safety deserve neither liberty nor safety." These kinds of advisors illustrate the peril of our nation and society. They have rejected Bible doctrine. They have rejected national strength. They have rejected divine viewpoint. They have embraced humanism, socialism, and other apostasies. "How long, ye simple ones, will ye love simplicity? And the scorners delight in the scorning, and fools hate knowledge?"

Seeking God's Blessing

The section of Proverbs that has just been under consideration has been harsh. In it we have seen the society given over to old sin natures. There has been a glimpse of the cycling of increasing troubles. But the Psalmist says, "His mercy endureth forever." At the end of this severe portion of Proverbs dealing with national destiny, we find ample indication of God's mercies:

> *But whoso hearkeneth unto me shall dwell safely,*
> *And shall be quiet from fear of evil.*
> *Proverbs 1:33*

This is a promise and, since Immutability is one of the characteristics of God's essence, we know that He can never go back on His Word. God will always protect and bless the nation that is sponsored and upheld by believers who "hearkeneth unto" Bible doctrine.

Just as God has set down the criterion for cursing, so He has set down a criterion for blessing. It is possible to make a general list of conditions which form the basis for national blessing. There are six general areas of conduct which God honors.

First of all, God evaluates a nation's determination to defend its divine national life, from business and politics to entertainment and the arts.

Christians should have shining Edification Complexes,* thus reflecting and drawing attention to the glory of God. Only then will they make other men truly desire to participate in the Christian Way of Life.

Salty Christians will always have their priorities in order. They will know that their first priority is evangelism, both at home and abroad. They will present the gospel at home through personal evangelism and support of their local church, and they will sponsor foreign missions as well.

Finally, a Christian should never fail to recognize his unique advantage for serving his country, his ability to pray to the sovereign Lord of Hosts on behalf of his nation and its leaders. Even the most seemingly insignificant Christian has a potential that a non-Christian lacks, no matter how important he may seem in the world's eyes. We can communicate with God and He will listen and respond. If we do not fulfill our mission as salt we ourselves are partly to blame if the nation does not receive God's blessing.

We must remember that spiritual muscle is the true key to national preservation. In the years following the Babylonian Captivity, many Jews were hesitant to leave the physical prosperity and thick walls of Babylon to return to the ruined, undefended city of Jerusalem. However, in a vision to His servant Zechariah, God made a promise to those Jews which can also be claimed by Christians today, "For I, saith the Lord, will be unto it a *wall* of fire round about, and will be the *glory* in the midst of it." (Zechariah 2:5) So although they would have no walls and no economy, God promised them both security and glory if they put their trust in Him. The wrath of God is indeed a terrible and fearsome thing, but His love and mercy are beautiful beyond all description.

CHAPTER VII

Proverbs of Leadership

These are also proverbs of Solomon,
Which the men of Hezekiah king of Judah copied out.
It is the glory of God to conceal a thing:
But the honour of kings is to search out a matter.
The heaven for height, and the earth for depth,
And the heart of kings is unsearchable.
Take away the dross from the silver,
And there shall come forth a vessel for the finer.
Take away the wicked from before the king,
And his throne shall be established in righteousness.
Proverbs 25:1-5

THE PRINCIPLES OF SUCCESSFUL RULERSHIP apply to anyone in a position of authority; they help you to rule yourself, your family, your business, a church or a government. Chapter 25 of Proverbs, as well as Chapters 26 - 29, constitute what we call "Hezekiah's Proverbs". They were written more than two centuries before Hezekiah's reign, but they had been filed away and were rarely read or studied until their republication in the 8th Century B.C. For this reason, verse one says,

These are also the proverbs of Solomon,

Which the men of Hezekiah king of Judah copied out.
Proverbs 25:1

During Hezekiah's kingship, the capital city of Jerusalem faced a severe crisis. The Assyrian armies, under King Sennacherib, were besieging the city because Hezekiah had refused to pay his annual tribute. The Assyrian army was invincible. The Jews' attempts to find an ally in Egypt had failed. Egypt, who had originally encouraged Jerusalem to rebel against Assyria, decided to make her own stand along the Sinai Peninsula. Egypt offered sympathy, but little more.

Hezekiah's State Department was dominated by cowards, fickle advisors whose only resource was human viewpoint.* The leadership obviously needed better counsel, and fortunately somebody remembered that in the archives were some of Solomon's writings on the means of successful ruling.

These chapters of Proverbs were brought out, copied (duplicated) and distributed to the king as well as to the people. Hezekiah and his subjects responded to the doctrine; their courage was revived, and as a result God miraculously spared the city. 185,000 Assyrian soldiers died on a single night after a visitation by the "angel of the Lord." Solomon's principles are not for mere academic curiosity; they really work. They helped Hezekiah maintain sound judgment and stability during a difficult crisis, and eventually they influenced him to initiate a revival in his kingdom.

The Successful Leader

The first proverb is a comparative-antithetical distich. It is comparative in the sense that Solomon is trying to bring out a contrast. And it is antithetical in that it compares God's modus operandi* with man's, the two being opposite in manner.

It is the glory of God to conceal a thing:
But the honor of kings is to search out a thing.
Proverbs 25:2

The "glory of God" is His character which is described in Chapter II, "The Wages of Wisdom." One of His characteristics is omniscience, which is an important quality in His role as King of Kings. God finds it wise to conceal things at certain times. On the other hand, human rulers can only be effective if they bring facts out into the open, "search out a thing," so that maximum understanding can be achieved.

God's knowledge is infinite, His righteousness is unimpeachable, and, consequently, His authority is unquestionable. His decisions do not need to be explained or justified to His subjects. A human ruler's knowledge factor, in comparison, is always finite. He is always subject to errors of misjudgment or misunderstanding. Therefore, it is to his credit to "search out" and reveal facts when he makes any decision.

The word "thing" in the Hebrew is *dabar*, pronounced *davar*, which means a point of doctrine. God occasionally hides certain points of doctrine from us. He hides certain facts about the future in order to avoid confusing people. For instance, in the Old Testament, Daniel was told by God to "seal the book, even to the time of the end." (Daniel 12:4) Apparently the Book of Daniel will never be completely understood until the very last days. In the New Testament, Christ told His disciples that no man knew the day or hour of His Second Coming, only the Father in Heaven. (See Matthew 24:36) Later, Paul refers to the principles of the Church Age as "mysteries" because they were hidden from the Old Testament believers. (Colossians 1:25-27) These are just a few examples of future things which God has hidden from us.

God also hides some things from certain types of people. "Though the Lord be high, yet hath he respect unto the lowly; but the proud he knoweth afar off." (Psalms 138:6) What God reveals to the humble, He may conceal from an arrogant person. (Matthew 11: 25) Even a believer can be left "in the dark" concerning divine viewpoint* if he is proud, because perception of truth depends on faith, not on human intelligence.

God may also choose not to reveal a certain doctrine until it is really important to a particular believer. For instance, a young man may never hear the Doctrine of Dying Grace* until just before he is being sent to battle. If he had heard it earlier he would probably have reacted just like most other young people when they hear of death, "I'm not going to die for at least 50 years, so I don't need to listen to this." God knows the perfect time to reveal a "thing" for the maximum benefit of each individual.

A contrast is seen when we turn from the divine ruler, God, to a human ruler, a "king" and his "honor," or human success. A human ruler must never fail to search out all the facts of a matter.

He may show favoritism otherwise, or simply poor judgment in discerning which of two alternative stories, if either, is true.

Leadership is not a position to be sought merely for the prestige that lies therein. It contains serious responsibilities which should never be taken lightly. Any Christian leader has three major areas of responsibility. First, he is responsible to God. No matter how highly placed you may be on Earth, you are still answerable to a higher authority, the soverign King of Kings. All earthly positions of leadership are ordained by God, so we should always realize who is ultimately responsible for our promotions. Secondly, leaders must learn the divine principles of leadership in order to rule wisely. Hence, they are responsible to learn and live Bible doctrine. The third responsibility of every Christian leader is toward his commission as an ambassador for Christ. He must always be aware of the fact that he personally represents Jesus Christ, whether he be a pastor, a parent, a husband, a supervisor, a teacher, or a coach. No matter how successful one has been in the past, or is at present, he must constantly recognize that he is anchored in a plan far greater than himself. Let his cry be David's, "Lead me to the rock that is higher than I." (Psalms 61:2) A leader who keeps in mind these three areas of responsibility should be a fair, honest, and respected leader and of great benefit to his subjects.

The Mysterious Leader

Verse three is a comparative distich which teaches a ruler the secret to dignity and poise.

> *The heaven for height, and the earth for depth,*
> *And the heart of kings is unsearchable.*
> *Proverbs 25:3*

The last verse taught us that a king must be very open in his duties towards his subjects. In contrast, this verse suggests that he maintain an aura of mystery about his private life. He must not divulge his personal thoughts and prejudices to his subjects.

We have two illustrations of mysteries to give us an idea of what a ruler should be: the heavens above and the earth below. Although we know much more about our physical environment than did the men of Solomon's time, our knowledge of the space above our heads and of the Earth beneath our feet is still far from complete. Many things remain hidden from us. Similarly, the private thoughts of leaders should be hidden from the public.

If a ruler exposes himself completely to his people, they may use the knowledge they have of his private life to take advantage of him. They may bribe, pressure or coerce him into favoring them when he makes decisions. If he remains somewhat aloof, people can be more assured that his decisions are objective, based on principles rather than emotion.

The Well-Advised Leader

The last two proverbs dealt directly with the qualities of the ruler himself. The next one deals with those men who are most closely associated with the king, his advisors. Any serious study of history reveals the significant influences that subordinate men have had in the course of world affairs. For instance, Queen Victoria gave her name to an entire era, but in actuality the accomplishments of the Victorian Period were largely the work of her two great Prime Ministers, Benjamin Disraeli and William Gladstone.[1] Everyone knows about the tragic period of the Spanish Inquisition under Ferdinand and Isabella, but not many people realize that the real force behind it was a fanatical priest, Thomas de Torquemada, Isabella's confessor and spiritual advisor.[2] No leader is entirely self-sufficient, hence, the importance of carefully chosen advisors. A stable leadership leads to a stable nation.

> *Take away the dross from the silver,*
> *And there shall come forth a vessel for the finer.*
> *Take away the wicked from before the king,*
> *And his throne shall be established in righteousness.*
> *Proverbs 25:4-5*

The above two verses form a parabolic tetrastich, the first two lines giving the figurative analogy, and the last two lines giving the real principle.

---

[1]G. M. Trevelyan, *A Shortened History of England*, Baltimore, Maryland: Penguin Books, 1942, pp. 511-524.

[2]William Hickling Prescott, *History of the Reign of Ferdinand and Isabella*, New York: The Heritage Press, 1962, pp. 81-83.

For his analogy, Solomon looks to the field of metalurgy. The Hebrew verb here translated "take away" refers to reduction by a melting process, and the "dross" is the refuse or the impurities in the silver ore. Only after ore has been refined can a smith fashion it into a truly beautiful "vessel." This process of refinement is then likened to the purging of the "wicked from before the king." "Before the king" is a technical term for those who are immediately under the king, his advisors or Cabinet. Any ruler who listens to wicked advice is going to be a failure, and his subjects will suffer.

Hezekiah had a particularly "wicked" advisor in his State Department during the Assyrian Crisis, Shebna. (Isaiah 36:3) Shebna was an ambitious and stylish coward. He was frightened by the blasphemy and threats of the Assyrian, Rabshakeh, so he advised Hezekiah to quit trusting in Jehovah and look to Egypt for help, or consider surrender. Of course surrender to Assyria would have meant slavery. Rather than concerning himself with maintaining his freedom, Shebna was building his tomb, so he could at least be buried in style. Shebna and his associates were obviously incapable of advising Hezekiah objectively. They were concerned more with personal welfare than with the welfare of their national entity, the first priority for any national leader.[3]

Fortunately, Hezekiah regarded the proverbs of Solomon and dismissed these poor advisors. Then he called for the Prophet Isaiah who reassured Hezekiah, "Be not afraid," he said, for the Lord had promised, "I will defend this city, to save it." (II Kings 19:6, 34) The nineteenth chapter of II Kings goes on to describe how God did spare Jerusalem. Hezekiah and his city survived to provide a marvelous example of the security promised to those who put their trust in the Lord. A nation was saved because of a stable leader who listened to good advisors.

We have used the example of a national leader, but this principle also applies on the most elementary level as well, such as a believer ruling his own soul.

> *Blessed is the man that walketh not in the counsel of the*
> *ungodly,*
> *Nor standeth in the way of sinners,*

---

[3]Micah 7:4 also describes Shebna and his "City Hall Crowd."

Nor sitteth in the seat of the scornful.
But his delight is in the law of the Lord;
And in his law doth he meditate day and night.
And he shall be like a tree planted by the rivers of water,
That bringeth forth his fruit in his season;
His leaf also shall not wither;
And whatsoever he doeth shall prosper.
Psalms 1:1-3

As this passage from Psalms points out, the individual who listens to the "counsel of the ungodly" regarding his public or private life is in just as much trouble as the king who listens to wicked advisors. However, if instead he hearkens to the "law of the Lord," the result will be prosperity, just as it will be for the king whose "throne shall be established in righteousness." (Proverbs 16:12)

How to Pray for Leaders

We should be concerned with the quality of our national leadership, because no social group can survive without competent people in charge. Paul reminds us of this duty in I Timothy,

I exhort therefore, that, first of all, supplications,
prayers, intercessions, and giving of thanks, be made for
all men; For kings, and for all that are in authority; that
we may lead a quiet and peaceable life in all godliness
and honesty. For this is good and acceptable in the sight
of God our Saviour; Who will have all men to be saved,
and to come unto the knowledge of the truth.
I Timothy 2:1-4

As Christians our prayers for men in authority in politics, education, or business should be directed toward four areas.

1. We should pray for their salvation. The first priority with any individual is the state of his soul, for unbelievers can never understand, let alone apply, divine principles. (I Corinthians 2:14)

2. Secondly, we should pray for their enlightenment by divine viewpoint* such as that we have just studied in Proverbs. In order to face the inevitable crises of leadership, leaders need to be stable and mature, qualities which are nurtured by Bible doctrine.

3. A third concern is for their safety, a factor which is particularly relevant in 20th Century America where political assassinations have become all too common. If we see that a particular man is doing a commendable job, we should pray that God will protect him, for we know that Satan will do everything in his power to subvert the work of people living according to the Divine Plan.

4. If we are *sure* that a man in authority is "wicked" or "ungodly," we have every right to pray for his removal. This prayer should be given as an alternative if the first two requests are answered negatively. We should exercise this request with the greatest discretion, first making sure that we are being truly objective and impersonal in our evaluation of the man in question.

We would undoubtedly see far greater leadership in our nation if we as Christians persistently interceded before the Throne of Grace in behalf of our country and its leaders. This kind of positive action is much to be preferred to the kind of vindictive "speaking evil of dignitaries" that we hear all too often. Since our nation is in dire need of God's grace, perhaps more now than at any other time in our national history, we should heed the exhortation of Zechariah to those Jews who survived the infamous Babylonian Captivity,

> Ask ye of the Lord rain in the time of the latter rain; so
> the Lord shall make bright clouds, and give them show-
> ers of rain, to every one grass in the field.
> Zechariah 10:1

Zechariah urged his people to pray for rain, here symbolic of national blessing and prosperity. The success of evangelism is dependent upon national stability and individual freedom. Hence we have a great stake in the quality of our national leadership. Our leaders are the men in the position to perpetuate our freedoms or lose them completely to Communism, internationalism, or anarchy. We have a righteous cause, and so we should not fail to beseech God to dispense grace to our troubled land.

Conclusion

In summary, we have studied three basic principles of leadership:

1. Human rulers should carefully investigate all the facts about a matter before making a decision.

2. Leaders should keep their private thoughts and desires hidden.

3. Leaders should protect themselves from bad advisors.

These three principles apply on some level to every person reading this book. You may be ruler of your own person, your children, your wife, your fellow workers, your employees, your congregation, your students, or your country. Whatever your level of authority, these doctrines can help both you and those under your authority to attain happiness and stability.

CHAPTER VIII

Proverbs for Personal Relationships

Put not forth thyself in the presence of the king,
And stand not in the place of great men:
For better it is that it be said unto thee,
  Come up hither,
Than that thou shouldest be put lower
  In the presence of the prince whom thine eyes have seen.
Go not forth hastily to strive,
Lest thou know not what to do in the end thereof,
When thy neighbour hath put thee to shame,
And thine infamy turn not away.
A word fitly spoken is like
  Apples of gold in pictures of silver,
As an earring of gold, and an ornament of fine gold,
So is a wise reprover upon an obedient ear.
As the cold of snow in the time of harvest,
So is a faithful messenger to them that send him;
For he refresheth the soul of his masters.
Whoso boasteth himself of a false gift is
Like clouds and wind without rain.
Proverbs 25:6-14

THE HEALTHY SOUL HAS two primary areas of interchange, one with God and the other with fellow members of the human race. In this chapter we are going to study a section of Proverbs which deals with the communications between people. There are many levels of communication, proceeding from the most intimate to the most casual. Each individual relates to his spouse, his family, friends, working companions, and fellow citizens. Proverbs 25 has some basic rules that can enable every type of human relationship to operate successfully.

Relating with Humility

Put not forth thyself in the presence of the king,
And stand not in the place of great men;
For better it is that it be said unto thee,
Come up hither,
Than that thou shouldest be put lower
In the presence of the prince whom thine eyes have seen.
Proverbs 25:6-7

The basic principle of the above verses is that we are not to attempt to promote ourselves by presuming to be intimate with our superiors. Children call this sort of behavior trying to be "teacher's pet." Solomon's principle of humility, if applied with honesty and patience, will in the end exhalt you. The failure to apply this principle implies pride, arrogance, and lust for power or human approbation.

God promotes humble men in time, but He always ignores the proud. This is why Paul says, "Mind not high things, but condescend to men of low estate. Be not wise in your own conceits." (Romans 12:16) One of the primary evidences of spirituality is humility. Every adult has some relationships in which he is subservient, and some in which he has authority. Even the humblest laborer has authority over his family. And his wife, though she is in submission to her husband, has authority over her children. If we humbly accept our positions of submission, then we will more likely succeed in our positions of authority.

The practical reason for the warning in verse 6 is given in verse

7. It is better to accept a secondary position, and then be promoted in due process, than to attempt to get in good with your superior and be rebuked for your presumptuousness. This is embarrassing, and embarrassed people seldom have inner happiness or exterior dignity.

New Testament Parallel

It is interesting to notice that many of Christ's parables are similar to the teachings of Proverbs. This is true of these last two verses. A similar lesson is found in Luke.

> *When thou are bidden by any man to a wedding, sit not down in the highest room; lest a more honorable man than thou be bidden of him. And him that bade thee and him come and say to thee, Give this man place; and thou begin with shame to take the lowest room. But when thou art bidden, go and sit down in the lowest room that, when he that bade thee cometh, he may say unto thee, Friend, go up higher; then shalt thou have worship (praise, glory) in the presence of them that sit at meat with thee. For whosoever exhalteth himself shall be abased; and he that humbleth himself shall be exalted.*
> *Luke 14:8-11*

Just as today, where the more important guests at a banquet sit nearest the head of the table, so in the ancient world, the most important guests dined in the highest "rooms." A proud man may march presumptuously to the highest place of honor because he thinks himself too good to eat in the lower rooms. However, he may also be asked to give up his place to someone who is truly deserving of the position of honor, a humiliating experience. But, if he had first gone to the lower rooms and then later been invited to a higher position by the host he could truly be honored. Furthermore he would "have worship (praise) in the presence of them that sat at meat with" him. This means that he would be accepted and respected by the men around him rather than resented as a haughty intruder, as would be the case with the proud men.

Society is built on a series of chain-of-command situations. When a person on the bottom seeks to supersede the person above him, he corrupts society. He also corrupts rapport love* between himself, his peers, and his superior. Both God and man appreciate and promote the man who stays in his place until he has earned the right to promotion. But the proud, pushy individual does not earn respect or love; consequently, if he is a Christian, any potential testimony he may attempt is ruined. If a child tries to grab authority in a family, that family suffers. If students try to run a school, the school will suffer. What is worse, there will be no basis for rapport love between the parents and children or teachers and students.

The promotion of self has no place in the divine plan. Under the subject of humility, Christ serves as the prime example. Christ, who was deity, humbled himself to become a common man,

> Made himself of no reputation, and took upon him the form of a servant, and was made in the likeness of men; . . . he humbled himself and became obedient unto death, even the death of the cross. Wherefore, God also hath highly exalted him, and given him a name which is above every name.
> Philippians 2:7-9

Because of his humility, Christ has been promoted above every other creature in the universe. His time to appear and function as King of Kings awaits only God's timetable. It has been prophesied and is sure to come. If we truly want our Edification Complex* to reflect the glory of God, we must reject pride, because "the pride of life, is not of the Father, but is of the world." (I John 2:16) We must go to the bottom of the table and wait for such promotion as God, or our human superior, determines.

Relating in Harmony

> Go not forth hastily to strive,
> Lest thou know not what to do in the end thereof,
> When thy neighbor hath put thee to shame.

> Debate thy cause with thy neighbor himself,
> And discover not a secret to another,
> Lest he that heareth it put thee to shame,
> And thine infamy turn not away.
> Proverbs 25:8-10

Most people (yes, even many Christians) occasionally talk too much. The most basic prerequisite of relating harmoniously with people is the knowledge of how to handle controversy, because controversy is inevitable in human relationships. Even the most loving husband and wife or the most equitable business relationships will sometimes have to face the tensions of disagreement.

The first line of verse 8 is a simple command, 'Do not be eager to argue.' The result too often may be that you are "put . . . to shame." Some people are so subjective that they cannot let the slightest offense go by without making a major issue of it. They have no long-suffering, they can never consider any extenuating circumstances in operation behind the actions of their offender. All they can see is that they have been unjustly treated and they want revenge. Such people often lose the very debates they initiate. There are two reasons for this: (1) the debate reveals that they really received no offense worth making an issue over, or (2) since such people are emotional and subjective, they usually make very poor debaters; they cannot put forth a good case for themselves. Consequently, a man emerges looking like a fool, which does very little to improve his already poor mental attitude. Here again, Bible doctrine, learned and applied, can rescue one from a damaging blow to his soul. In knowing the doctrine of harmony, one can 'head off at the pass' this troublesome activity. Even if we are already guilty, this Proverb can rebuke us, causing us to repent, and correct and instruct us against future foolishness.

New Testament Parallel

In the Sermon on the Mount, Christ warned against retaliation.

I say unto you that ye resist not evil, but whosoever shall smite thee on thy right cheek, turn to him the other also. And if any man will sue thee at the law, and take away thy coat, let him have thy cloak also.
Matthew 5:39-40

There is no room in the Church for trouble-makers. If we quarrel with unbelievers we destroy our witness to them. If we quarrel with fellow believers we harm the unity that we are supposed to have in Christ.[1] It is for this reason that Paul described a harsh treatment for trouble-makers,

Now I beseech you, brethren, mark them *who cause divisions and offenses contrary to the doctrine which ye have learned; and* avoid them.
Romans 16:17

To avoid being ostracized and put to shame, we must remain "slow to speak, slow to wrath." (James 1:19)

If You Must Debate, Do It Privately

Verses 9 and 10 recognize that sometimes confrontations are unavoidable. Some differences are too great to be ignored, but even then, third parties should not be involved. We should isolate our controversy and try to handle it in a one-to-one situation. Hence, Solomon writes, "Discover not a secret to another." The "secret" is the quarrel itself. The more people involved in a quarrel, the fuzzier the issues become. Just as no two witnesses will report an accident in the same way, so no two outsiders will understand a disagreement in the same way. The more people you involve in a debate, the greater the potential damage it can do. Civilization runs on teamwork. Anytime you split up a team, be it a family, a church, or a nation, you are courting disaster.

It is always a temptation to go to one's friends for reassurance and support. However, every support gathered by one side will probably be matched by one on the opposition's side, and the number of people involved does not change the basic facts of the original quarrel. Additional people only muddy the waters and probably bring in false or irrelevant issues which add fuel to what may initially have been a small fire. If two individuals find their differences irreconcilable they can quietly ignore one another, but if large numbers of people get involved, there is usually the break-up of a major social unit causing *temporary* chaos and *permanent* resentment. Several people on one side can constantly reinforce the hatred that led to the split, whereas two individuals may more easily forget their private differences.

---

[1]"So we, being many, are one body in Christ, and every one members one of another." Romans 12:5

Verse 10 reveals another reason for not sharing your quarrels. If you try to enlist some knowledgeable people to your cause, they will recognize your error and apply Romans 16:17. They will recognize that *you* are out of line and so not only will you fail to gain support for your present quarrel, but you will get a bad reputation, "infamy," as a trouble-maker. Once again you will end up being ostracized.

Everyone seeks happiness, but people who are embarrassed, put to shame, or lonely are not happy. God always has perfect happiness and He wishes us to reflect it as part of our Edification Complex*. It is to God's glory, as well as our own benefit, that we heed the following words:

> If it be possible, as much as lieth in you, live peaceably with all men.
> Romans 12:18

Relating Through Helpfulness

Advice

One of the best ways to relate favorably to other people is to be helpful. The first method of helpfulness we will discuss is the giving of advice. So many people make a nuisance of themselves by always giving advice, that the word has almost come to have a bad connotation. Someone who gives too much advice faces the same situation as the boy who is always crying "Wolf!" People stop taking him seriously. However, the truly wise person who can dispense advice on occasion and with sensitivity, tact and discretion will always be respected and sought after.

> A word fitly spoken is like
> Apples of gold in pictures of silver.
>
> As an earring of gold, and an ornament of fine gold,
> So is a wise reprover upon an obedient ear.
> Proverbs 25:11-12

The illustration given in this first parabolic distich is one which may mean little to readers today. "Apples of gold in pictures of silver," or more correctly "apples of gold on trays of silver," is an ancient symbol of a decorative item for the home to indicate wealth and success.² Hence if we can give advice at the proper time, we beautify and enrich a person's life.

A "word fitly spoken" is divine viewpoint* corresponding to the need of the recipient. There are many categories of doctrine that you could apply at different times. Perhaps it could be a *warning*. You may have a friend who is in danger of becoming a troublemaker such as Solomon described in verses 8-10. In that case he needs to be warned of the potential consequences of his actions. Maybe you know someone in need of *assurance*; an acquaintance of yours may be doubting his salvation or doubting God's ability to take care of him. You should then be able to give the doctrine of Eternal Security or the doctrine of the Essence of God.³ There may be times when a "word fitly spoken" could be a point of *prophecy* for someone who is fearful of the future. There is a fit time to give the *gospel*, and we should be prepared to recognize the opportunity to evangelize when God gives it to us. You could know someone in need of *reproof*. This must be handled with extreme caution and only by someone with the authority to know his subject.

I am sure that every reader is anxious to be a giver of such needed advice as described above, BUT, just remember one thing! Every teacher has at one time been a student. No one should presume to have a mouth to speak until he has first had ears to hear. We have a faith that can transform society, but it must be disseminated by responsible, competent people who know what they are doing.

Verse 12 deals with the last type of advice mentioned above, *reproof*. The illustration is the enhancing effect of gold jewelry to the beauty of a woman. Solomon says that the ear which is obedient to reproof is as beautiful as golden earrings and ornaments adorning a lovely woman.

The phrase, "a wise reprover" in Hebrew is *hakach*. It is in

---

²A development of this symbol is found in Greek mythology. Golden apples were greatly valued by the gods. They were contained in the Garden of Atlas which was guarded by the Hesperides, a group of nymphs who were honored with this responsibility. Hence, a tray of golden apples became a symbol of a man's belief that he was blessed by the gods. Michael Grant, *Myths of the Greeks and Romans*, New York: New American Library, Inc., 1962, pp. 258-259.

³Chapter III, page 38.

the hiphil or causative stem which means that he causes someone
to be reproved by communicating a point of doctrine wisely. There
are four qualifications necessary in anyone who wishes to be a
reprover. *First,* he must know doctrine; he should not go around
advising people simply from human viewpoint*. *Secondly,* he
must himself be obedient to doctrine, "first cast the beam out of
thine own eye, and then shalt thou see clearly to cast the mote
out of thy brother's eye." (Matthew 7:5) *Thirdly,* he must be in a
chain-of-command position to reprove. Children, for instance,
are not in a position to reprove their parents, even though the
parents may be acting contrary to the will of God. Finally, the
reprover must always act from an attitude of humility. He must
not feel that he is giving reproof because of his own superior
moral position, but rather that he is merely explaining a divine
principle that operates immutably, regardless of how good or bad
he himself may be.

It is not easy to accept reproof; it takes a mature person to
allow another to point out his errors. Those lacking objectivity
will not look at the advice but rather will look at the adviser.
Rather than *responding* to the principle, they *react* to the speaker.
That is why the best means of giving reproof is in a public
speaking situation rather than in a one-on-one situation. In a
Bible class, for instance, a teacher can teach a general principle
and each listener can respond privately without the embarrass-
ment of a face-to-face encounter.

Service

The second type of helpfulness we will study is under the category of *service*, faithfulness in the performance of one's duties
under the chain-of-command.

> *As the cold of snow in the time of harvest,*
> *So is a faithful messenger to those who send him;*
> *For he refresheth the soul of his masters.*

> *Whoso boasteth himself of a false gift is*
> *Like clouds and wind without rain.*
> *Proverbs 25:13-14*

Anyone who has ever worked harvesting crops in the late
summer heat should appreciate the word-picture in verse 13.
There is no shade in the middle of a wheat field in July, the

work is strenuous, and the sun is unmerciful. Since plumbing and refrigeration in Solomon's time were not quite what they are today, cold tap water and ice cubes were an unknown quantity. So while the workers labored in the fields, the master would send a runner to the mountains to bring back fresh snow to refresh his men. The workers would be invigorated and refreshed and ready to back to work after a long drink of snow water.

The purpose of the physical picture of an icy drink during the heat of harvest time is to give some appreciation for the refreshment that a faithful servant brings to his master. If a supervisor gives a subordinate a job to do and later checks and finds that it has been done, he rejoices. He is happy and relaxed. He treats the rest of his men well, he is a better husband and father when he goes home at night, and he is more relaxed in his relationship with friends and neighbors. In other words, if one man does his job well he can have a positive effect on a large number of other human relationships.

The opposite side of the picture should be faced, too. If the supervisor had found the job unfinished, he would have been angry with the worker and anxious for himself because he was probably responsible to his own supervisor. Consequently, his relationships with his other men, his wife and children and his friends would all have suffered.

However, we are primarily concerned here with your immediate relationships with other people. How then does the worker's service affect his relationship with his supervisor? If he does not fulfill his duties he forfeits any basis for further relationship. The supervisor will be angry and distrustful. The faithful worker gains respect and admiration from his superior. He lays the foundation for future interaction. If, for instance, the worker is a Christian and the supervisor is not, faithful service is the best means of testimony available. The opposite character is described in verse 14.

"Clouds and wind" are a good sign of rain, always a welcome relief to the semi-arid Middle East. However, if a farmer saw "clouds and wind" and began to look forward to rain but none came, he would be extremely disappointed. Such is the reaction to a man who gives certain promises but never performs. He says he is a Christian, but he shows no love, no peace, no joy.

To raise someone's expectations by promising something that

you cannot or will not deliver is not simply careless, it is cruel as well. We must be willing to accept the responsibility of our promises, or else stop making them. To claim oneself a Christian is to accept the responsibility of being the salt of the earth. It includes the responsibility of exhibiting the fruits of the spirit: "Love, joy, peace, long-suffering, gentleness, goodness, faith, meekness, temperance." (Galatians 5:22-23)

Conclusion

In summary, we have three means of relating to other people: humility, harmony, and helpfulness. God has made us gregarious creatures; though we each need our periods of privacy, equally strong is our need to relate to fellow humans. Too often though, those relationships are soured by selfishness, immaturity, and subjectivity. If we can remember PROVERBS FOR PERSONAL RELATIONSHIPS we will increase the personal happiness of many and edify the lives of everyone we meet.

CHAPTER IX

The Essence of the Soul

THIS CHAPTER CONCERNS itself with the place in which wisdom is gathered and retained, the human soul. Common to each of the following selections from the Book of Proverbs is the Hebrew word *nephesh*. This word comes from the Hebrew verb *nephash* which means to breath, or in the passive, to be breathed upon. The noun *nephesh* is translated as *soul* in Proverbs 38 times, and as *heart* twice. The following verses illustrate the close relationship between wisdom and soul, a relationship somewhat similar to family and house.

> *For as he thinketh in his heart* (nephesh) *so is he;*
> *Eat and drink, saith he to thee;*
> *But his heart* (leb)[1] *is not with thee.*
> *Proverbs 23:7*

> *He that is of a proud heart* (nephesh) *stirreth up strife;*
> *But he that putteth his trust in the Lord shall be made fat.*
> *Proverbs 28:25*

[1] *Leb* in Proverbs 23:7 is used to connote the idea of the center of the emotions, sometimes the will and even the intellect. *Nephesh* is used to connote all of the mental faculties.

But whoso committeth adultery with a woman lacketh
understanding;
He that doeth it destroyeth his own soul. (nephesh).
Proverbs 6:32

Like the cold of snow in the time of harvest which cools
the air,
So is the faithful messenger to those who sent him;
*For he refreshes the soul (*nephesh*) of his masters.*
Proverbs 25:13

When wisdom entereth into thine heart (leb),
And knowledge is pleasant unto thy soul (nephesh),
Discretion shall preserve thee, understanding shall keep
thee.
Proverbs 2:10-11

He that getteth wisdom loveth his own soul (nephesh);
He that keepeth understanding shall find good.
Proverbs 19:8

The theme of Proverbs is that WISDOM is the principal thing. Wisdom is more than mere knowledge; it is exhibited by discretion and judgment which result from applied knowledge. This commodity is one which cannot be inherited and it cannot be purchased. It is the most important resource of society, much more valuable than bank accounts, credits or debt-free properties, commodities which are easily destroyed or dissipated. Wisdom is repeatedly taught as the principal thing. While it cannot be inherited or purchased, it can be gathered and cultivated. Wisdom is like a flower that needs a receptive soul in which to take root.

Some flowers grow marvelously when the proper environment is available. Flowers will either be stunted or will completely die if the environment is not sympathetic to their needs. So we will find it helpful to understand the optimum "environment" of wisdom.

However, there are different kinds of souls encountered in the Book of Proverbs. Some people develop generous souls while others develop greedy souls (Proverbs 11:25). There are sweet souls and bitter souls (Proverbs 13:19). We encounter refreshing souls and stagnant souls (Proverbs 25:14). We find industrious souls and idle souls (Proverbs 19:15) Even as a plot of ground may grow either flowers or weeds, so the human soul can be the generating place for wisdom, but also for its antithesis, foolishness.

The word "soul"[2] is used frequently in Christian circles, but usually in a vague manner. Most people would be hard-pressed to come up with a clear definition. Before the specific doctrines contained in Proverbs can have optimum effect, they must be conveyed into the soul (nephesh) of a believer and become established there. Therefore it is important that we have some categorical knowledge of the essence and function of man's soul.

In Genesis 2:7, we learn that God's hand was the agent of man's beginning. God formed the human body to be the earthly home of man's soul. Then God breathed into that body the "breath of life," literally the plural form, "lives." Through this means, the first man, Adam, became a "living soul." In order for man to function as an earthly creature, God gave physical life to the body he created. At the same time, He added a kind of life not possessed by all His other creatures. God gave man a living spirit as well as a living body. This explains the use of the plural form of life mentioned above. This is to define "soul life" as the unique combination of physical and spiritual life in one creature, man.

Man's "living soul" was created "in the image of God," the implication being of a shadow image rather than a concrete image. With the possession of a soul, man became a unique creation, different from angelic life and different from animal life.

While angels have only spiritual life and animals only have physical life, man has both. That unique combination constitutes the meaning of the word "soul". Although the soul survives physical death, either in heaven or hell, it does not begin until physical birth. In eternity, the believer's soul will enjoy a new body, far surpassing the body of clay.

The "soul" has a spiritual essence. The first man, Adam, had three kinds of life. His body possessed *physical life* with which he was conscious of his physical environment (what we call loosely the earth). Adam was also given a *living spirit* similar to God's.[3]

---

[2]Another discussion of the soul or *nephesh* may be found in an essay by W. Hewitt Tier entitled "Theories About Life and It's Origin," *Symposium on Creation III*, Grand Rapids: Baker Book House, 1971.

[3]"God is a spirit, and they that worship him must worship in spirit and in truth." John 4:24

Spirit life is eternal and is unique to God, angels and man. With his spirit, Adam became conscious of God, his Creator. The third kind of life, *soul life,* belongs to man exclusively since it denotes the combination of physical and spiritual life. Through SOUL LIFE, man becomes self-conscious; he becomes aware of his particular existence as being between heaven and earth, and between past and future, "a little lower than the angels," but having "dominion over . . . the beasts."[4] The body has an essence which can be categorically described, i.e., bone (skeletal system), flesh (muscular system), blood (circulatory system), etc. So also the soul has an essence which we must learn about if we are to appreciate the magnificent banquet of "soul-food" available to sustain our soul in Proverbs.

A modest detour is in order at this point. Before considering the essence of the soul, it is necessary to orient to the problem that sin has caused in the soul. When Adam consciously chose to eat of the Tree of the Knowledge of Good and Evil (which was the only way he could sin at that time), he committed the sin of disobedience. He then became aware of the difference between good and evil through his wrong choice. Consequently, Adam's spirit, that part of his being which was most like God, died. It was that spirit which enabled Adam to know and appreciate his Creator. When it died, a vast change came over the soul of Adam. He promptly began to misunderstand both his relationship with God and his purpose for existence. His soul fell under the domination of sin and Satan.

At this point, man acquired what is described in our particular terminology as an "old sin nature" which usurped the Creator's place of lordship in the soul of man. Figure 5 illustrates.

Man estranged himself from God, and could never have experienced further relationship with God through his own efforts. Fortunately, God did not leave man completely at the mercy of his sinful nature, but provided a means of salvation.[5] However, the message of salvation is not the message of Proverbs. Proverbs is written to give divine viewpoint* to one who is already a believer, one whose soul has already been "saved" by God, recon-

---

[4] Psalms 8:5-7

[5] Genesis 3:15, John 3:16, 18, 36, and Acts 2:8, 4:12.

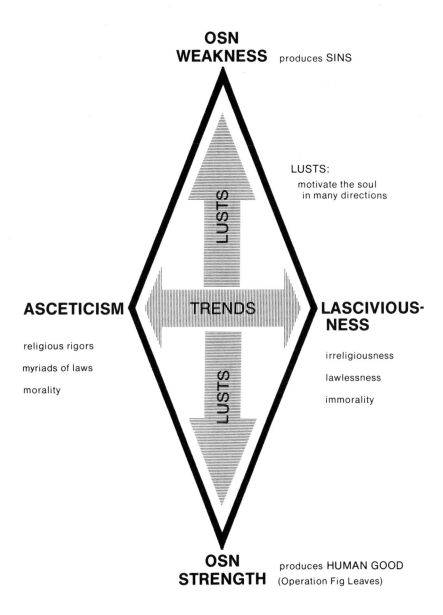

Old Sin Nature (OSN)_____Figure **5**

ciled through God's plan of salvation.[6] To benefit most from Proverbs, one's human spirit must receive the life-giving power of the Holy Spirit.[7] Figure 6 illustrates.

Principles in the Proverbs can be of some value to anyone who adheres to them. Many non-believers do in part heed the wisdom of Proverbs regarding mental attitudes and human relationships and they experience soulish benefits. However, the greatest benefit is reserved for those whose souls have been saved through faith in Jesus Christ, and who are enlightened to receive the divine viewpoint of life. Divine viewpoint is cloudy and is never really clear to those who lack faith. Faith is a non-meritorious system of perception, God's sovereign means of communicating truth to man.

We may now examine the part of man's soul which can be lost forever from God, or experience eternal life with God, depending on how each individual decides, (with his human volition). The soul consists of six different but related components or facets. (See Figures 7 and 8).

Mentality

The Lord by wisdom hath founded the earth;
By understanding hath he established the heavens.
Proverbs 3:19

The first and most important facet of the soul is Mentality (intelligence), man's power to reason. With his Mentality, man can assimilate, categorize, memorize, and systematize data. The Mentality of the natural or non-regenerate man concerns itself primarily with physical and social phenomena. Any interest in

---

[6] Acts 16:31 and II Corinthians 5:19

[7] "For the law of the Spirit of life in Christ Jesus hath made me free from the law of sin and death." Romans 8:2
"the things of God knoweth no man, but the Spirit of God. Now we have received, not the spirit of the world, but the spirit which is of God; that we might know the things that are freely given to us of God . . . But the natural man receiveth not the things of the Spirit of God: for they are foolishness unto him: neither can he know them, because they are spiritually discerned." I Corinthians 2:11b-12, 14

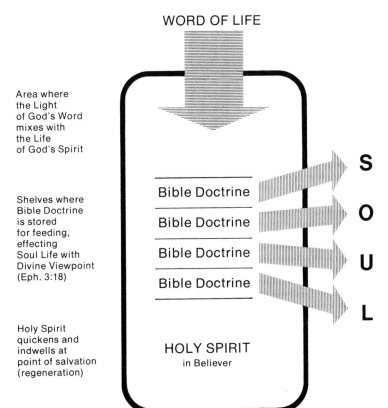

WORD OF LIFE

Area where
the Light
of God's Word
mixes with
the Life
of God's Spirit

Shelves where
Bible Doctrine
is stored
for feeding,
effecting
Soul Life with
Divine Viewpoint
(Eph. 3:18)

Bible Doctrine

Bible Doctrine

Bible Doctrine

Bible Doctrine

S
O
U
L

Holy Spirit
quickens and
indwells at
point of salvation
(regeneration)

HOLY SPIRIT
in Believer

Human Spirit (Believer)_____Figure **6**

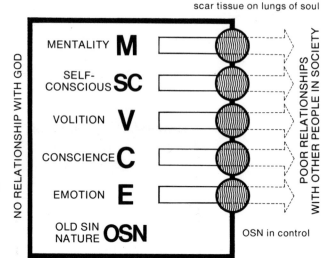

Soul in Body (Fallen Man) _____ Figure **7**

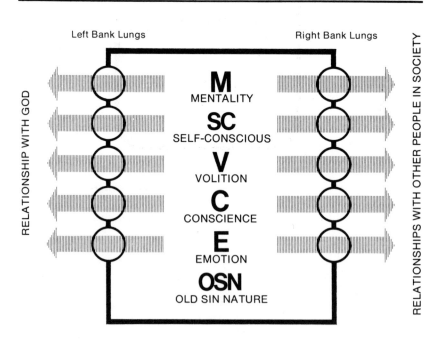

Soul in Body (Believer) _____ Figure **8**

spiritual phenomena is largely vague, merely academic and without eternal significance. Man's mentality is a marvellous thing, and he has the ability to discern the existence of his Creator. Yet this mentality remains, without spiritual life, an earthly capacity, and hence non-appreciative or little-appreciative of God. In fact, as I Corinthians 2:14 points out, the "things of the Spirit of God" are "foolishness" to the mentality of the natural man.

However, mentality begins to change when a man is spiritually reborn, reconciled to his Maker. He is made a "new creature; old things are passed away; behold all things are become new. And all things are of God . . ." (II Corinthians 5:17-18). His mentality gets a new pair of eyes, and becomes able to perceive and appreciate spiritual phenomena, primarily through the study of the Bible. The Mentality, or intelligence, is the KEY FACET of the soul since all data must pass first into the mind. Then data can be channeled into other parts of the soul.[8] (See Figures 9 and 10)

The Mentality, upon receiving data, first considers it and attempts to understand or absorb it. The Mentality will accept or reject the data through means of the reasoning power (frame of reference: is it true or false) and/or through means of the Conscience (frame of reference: is it good or bad). If accepted (Volition — exercise of the free will), the data will be categorized and appropriately stored in some shelf of the memory bank. It may become part of the conscious memory, and thus be recalled at a moment's notice. Other data goes into the sub-conscious shelf, where it may lie dormant only to be recalled through great effort or in moments of extreme passivity (e.g., dreams during sleep). This stored knowledge is called *gnosis*, knowledge in the soul's mentality. That part of *gnosis* which is spiritual truth revealed through God's Word, is now ready to be applied by faith. (See Figure No. 11)

[8]The Mentality has a Top Chamber, referred to in scripture as the mind. The mentality also has a bottom chamber, referred to in scripture as the heart. These will be considered in this chapter, and are illustrated in Figures 9, 10 and 11.

BIBLE DOCTRINE

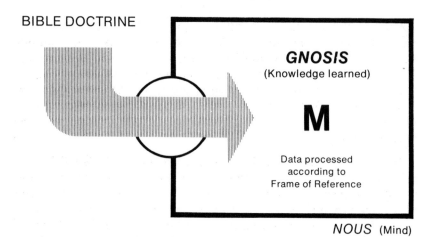

Mentality-Top Chamber_____Figure **9**

DIVINE VIEWPOINT

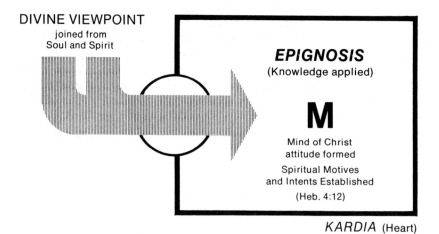

Mentality-Bottom Chamber_____Figure **10**

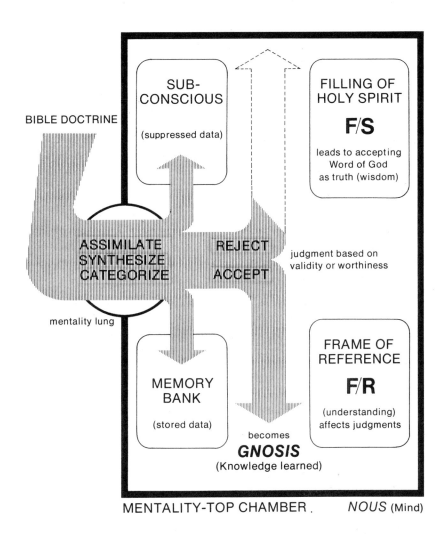

Mind at Work (Believer)_____Figure **11**

Self-Consciousness

My son, attend to my words;
Incline thine ear unto my sayings.
Let them not depart from thine eyes;
Keep them in the midst of thine heart.
Proverbs 4:20-21

The second facet of the soul of man is *Self-Consciousness*, making man aware of himself so that he can say with Descartes, "I think, therefore I am." It is through this facet that he relates personally to God, to fellow beings, and to the lower creation, flora and fauna. Because of his relationship to God, man is to recognize his Maker as the ultimate superior, Lord and Sovereign Master.

To his fellow homo sapiens, man relates as an equal, although he recognizes certain chain-of-command relationships such as government over citizen, parent over child, employer over employee, or teacher over student. To the lower creation, man assumes the position of master.

There is also angelic life which occasionally appeared to man in the Old Testament, but man was never to worship angels or to have any intimate personal relationships with them. Angels merely served as messengers from God and as such were treated with respect.

Volition

My son, forget not my law;
But let thine heart keep my commandments.
Proverbs 3:1

Third in line of importance in the soul is *Volition*, or Free Will. This facet is another reflection of man's being created in the image of God. Man is not an externally controlled robot. God created man with the privilege of making his own decisions and reaping the benefits or consequences of those decisions. This gives man the potential to exist in harmony or out of harmony with God's Plan, but does not force him to do either.

Man is then free to determine his eternal destiny as well as his earthly mode of operation. Volition gives man dignity, and a potential for greatness as well as potential for remarkable degradation. Under the function of Volition, man is free to choose either God's system of standards or some kind of humanistic system. In either case, man is *free* to choose.

Conscience

Withhold not good from them to whom it is due,
When it is in the power of thine hand to do it.
Proverbs 3:27

The fourth facet of the soul is *Conscience*. It is Conscience that determines the norms and standards which will govern man's thoughts and actions. Each soul possesses this warning system to guide and direct man. Of course, there are many systems of norms and standards besides the divine norms and standards taught by the Word of God. The Conscience can just as easily be governed by wrong standards as by right ones, but if the Biblical standards prevail, then man will be blessed under the sovereign Plan of God. Under the function of Volition, man is free to choose his own system of standards. And even though he accepts Biblical standards, he may disobey.

The Conscience then goes on Operation Guilt Complex until a man either repents of his sin and confesses it to God or else excuses his behavior via rationalism or the acceptance of some new system of standards. He may resort to such modern means of rationalism as "situation ethics" whereby the individual decides what is right for himself at a given time or in a given "situation." There is no adherence to any further authority than SELF, and his particular ambition at the moment. This rationale states that actions can only be determined as "right" or "wrong" in spontaneously specific situations rather than by God's eternal, immutable code. Man may choose a new system of norms and standards like the "New Morality" which maintains that each can do his own thing as long as he does not hurt anyone else. Under this system any form of sexual perversion may be excused if it is not forced on unconsenting persons. This illustrates how the Old Sin Nature distorts the Conscience. It may be interesting to observe that each of these world views, Situation Ethics and the New

Morality is egocentric or selfishly centered, about 180 degrees opposite to the Golden Rule, the New Testament ethic.

Emotion

Be not afraid of sudden fear,
Neither of the desolation of the wicked when it cometh.
For the Lord shall be thy confidence,
And shall keep thy foot from being taken.
Proverbs 3:25-26

The last facet of the soul is *Emotion*, which gives man the capacity to appreciate God and his fellow man, as well as many aspects of human life. Before the Fall, Adam knew only blessing because sin had not yet destroyed his soul. But with the advent of sin, his Emotion experienced frustration, as did the other facets of Adam's soul. Man's *Emotional Pattern* no longer appreciated his Maker and the *Conscience* stimulated guilt. No longer comfortable in God's presence, the *Volition* stimulated a migration out of Paradise to seek less guilt and more comfort. The *Mentality*, aware of the loss of righteousness, designed a kind of cover-up, in Adam's case fig leaves. Adam's location changed, his mode of operation changed, and his entire soul and purpose for living became distorted from its divine purpose. His soul could not recover until it was restored and regenerated by God Himself, through His plan of Grace.

In addition to (1) the soul's perversion, all men have inherited (2) a sinful nature from Adam (Romans 5:12, 15). Each soul can be restored through the regeneration of the Holy Spirit, called salvation. Salvation occurs in a single point of time with results that last forever, hence one's salvation can never be lost. (It is often preceded by a period of spiritual development, as birth is preceded by pregnancy). Conversion, which makes one a totally "new creature," begins at the point of salvation but continues over time to transform the whole man. "The law of the Lord (Bible doctrine) is perfect (complete), converting the SOUL." (Psalms 19:7).

God has provided a mechanism for this process which is described in terms analogous to physical breathing (See Figure 12). The believer inhales the *pneuma* or breath of God (His Word) into the lungs of the soul and then is progressively sanctified and "changed into the same image (of Christ) from glory to glory (from one level to the next), even as by the Spirit of the Lord." (II Corinthians 3:18) God wants His image to be reflected in the soul of the believer. This is only possible if the believer constantly inhales doctrine such as the invigorating, refreshing 'air' that is found in Proverbs.

Earlier we referred briefly to the two chambers of the Mentality. The Top Chamber is what the Bible calls the "mind" or in Greek, *nous*. It first receives doctrine for consideration and understanding (See Figure 4). In the Bottom Chamber of the Mentality, which the Bible calls the "heart" (in Greek, *kardia*), doctrine is transformed from mere academic knowledge to an attitude in the soul. It is in the consistent application of doctrine toward the patterns of thought and action that truth becomes wisdom. See Figure 11 where the activities of the soul and spirit are combined.

Figure 12 illustrates the effects of the operation of Spiritual breathing. As in physical breathing there comes a vibrancy, tone and energy to life, so it is in Spiritual breathing. Instead of strong muscles, endurance, color and vigor as with physical exercise, there begins to develop various qualities of the Spirit. This is called the Edification Complex. Figure 13 illustrates.

Only after the soul has turned its *gnosis* (knowledge) into *epignosis* (wisdom) does it acquire an Edification Complex.* This is evidenced by (1) Grace Orientation, (2) Capacity for Love, (3) Inner Happiness, (4) Spiritual Peace and (5) a Mastery over the Details of Life. An Edification Complex[9] is a reflection in the soul of the "mind of Christ," thus giving a believer a "sweet savor" toward God and an impact on his fellow man (See Figure 14).

Just as air follows a cycle whereby it is inhaled, the oxygen circulated and then exhaled as carbon dioxide, so doctrine also follows a cycle. By faith it is inhaled into the mind. The indwelling Holy Spirit reinforces the importance of the doctrine, and it is channelled to the "heart" to become

[9]The concept of Christian character is illustrated by the diagram of the Edification Complex as seen in Figure 14. It is discussed by Paul as the "fruit of the spirit" in Galatians 5:22-23. It is discussed by David and Solomon not as fruit but rather as a tree, a very productive tree. They say of wisdom, "She is a *tree of life* to them that lay hold upon her, and happy is every one that retaineth her." (Proverbs 3:18) This is also suggested in Proverbs 13:12 and 11:30.

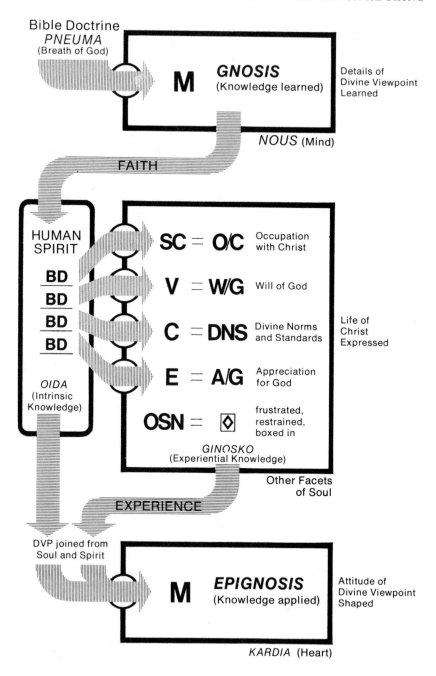

Spiritual Breathing_____Figure **12**

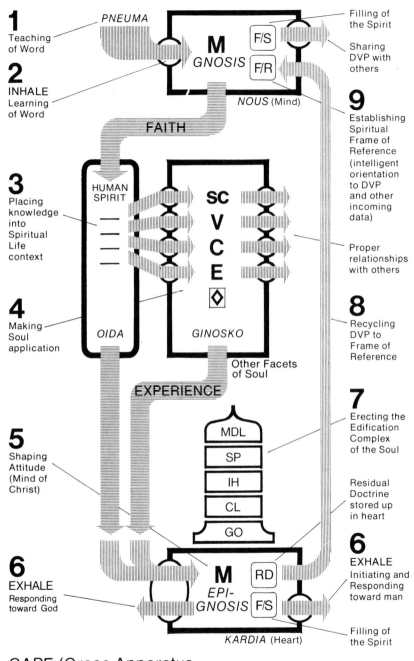

GAPE (Grace Apparatus
for Perception and Edification)_____Figure **13**

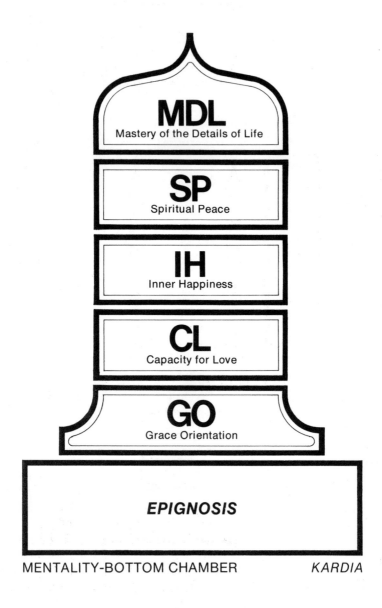

Edification Complex
(Taj Mahal of the Soul)_____Figure **14**

attitude, known as a "heart after God." Then the believer is able to "exhale" the results in his attitude to God and to man, and this develops a beautiful citadel of the soul, the Edification Complex.

There is no breathing in the womb. Similarly there is no soul life in the womb. The Mentality and the dormant Old Sin Nature are in the embryo from the moment of conception. This is the soul-format, but not soul-life. Soul-life itself only begins at the moment of physical birth. Since Adam could only produce after his own kind, he passed on his Old Sin Nature[10] which, in his children was also activated at the moment of birth. The Old Sin Nature is unrestricted in the newborn soul, and acquires potential mastery over the infant's life. Personal sin then becomes inevitable.

Only when an individual reaches the age of reason and can sense the reality of the existence of God is he accountable for those sins. If at any time during the remainder of his life he should hear the gospel of Jesus Christ and make a positive decision to trust Christ as Lord and Saviour, he will gain a power to neutralize or offset the power of his Old Sin Nature. That old nature will continue to struggle for dominance over the soul. But the "new man" will gain new strength to resist and dominate.

The Old Sin Nature is clever and is neither limited to overt personal sinfulness nor even mental-attitude sins. It can inspire such subtle perversions as the substitution of human good for divine good as a means of self-justification. Human good means nothing to God. But it often raises one's self-esteem as well as raises one's image in the eyes of other men. It often deludes an individual into a false set of values, and a false sense of righteousness. An example of this is "Operation Fig Leaf" in the Garden of Eden. When Adam recognized his sin, symbolized by his nakedness, he tried to cover it up with an apron of fig leaves. We have illustrated the Old Sin Nature in Figure 5. It has an area of weakness which produces sin. It also has an area of strength that produces "human good." Both products of the Old Sin Nature are repugnant to God. Jesus Christ died as an atonement for all the personal sins of all men,

---

[10]"Wherefore, as by one man sin entered into the world, and death by sin; and so death passed upon all men, for that all have sinned." Romans 5:12

*And he is the propitiation for our sins, and not for ours
only but also for the sins of the whole world.
I John 2:2*

At the same time, God rejected all "human good" as a system of
righteousness,

*Not by works of righteousness which we have done, but
according to his mercy he saved us, by the washing of
regeneration, and renewing of the Holy Spirit.
Titus 3:5*

Anyone who expects to survive God's final judgment will discover his utter insufficiency too late if he is depending on his
"human good," that is, no faith. Proverbs helps the believer to
discern the fallacy of relying on human good as a bona fide expression of the Christian Life.

The Old Sin Nature has numerous trends and lust patterns,
varied enough to attract all types of personalities. For instance,
in its area of weakness it has licentiousness, sexual perversions,
greed, envy, etc. Excesses of various kinds are expressed by
whatever type of lust pattern predominates in the Old Sin
Nature.

In its area of strength, the Old Sin Nature displays such trends
as asceticism, religion, ritualism and social welfare. Whichever
activity is followed, the more dignified or the less dignified, all
are products of the old nature and can only be neutralized by
Bible doctrine and the filling of the Spirit. Some of these systems
(social welfare for instance) are not wrong in concept, but only
when they are substituted for bona fide divine good and are mis-
represented as a means of justification.

This chapter has constructed a clinical concept of the essence
and function of man's soul. As we consider and apply the ideas and
principles in Proverbs, this knowledge of the soul should provide
us with a ready frame of reference to assimilate and categorize
knowledge. It shows the difference between knowledge and wisdom, a difference which might be correlated to the possession of
raw ingredients versus the possession of a finished product.

Wisdom is seen in the preserving of one's soul life by avoiding
those sins, such as adultery, which will guarantee the destruction
of the soul. (Proverbs 6:32) Wisdom is seen in the erection of an

edification complex, the grace which should characterize Christian living. Wisdom is also seen in the dissemination of knowledge, a dissemination which includes winning souls.

The fruit of the righteous is a tree of life;
And he that winneth souls is wise.
Proverbs 11:30

Solomon was a wise teenager who listened to the instruction of his father, King David. He was wise again in his early sixties when, after twenty years of decadent living, he rebounded and once again assumed the responsible management of his country. He was possibly the wisest of all, when, in his later sixties, he gathered a handful of scribes such as Ithiel and Ucal and published his writings, which include Ecclesiastes and Song of Solomon as well as the Proverbs. This endeavor, however late it happened in his life, ultimately had great impact upon souls in subsequent generations.

Like Solomon, David was a wise teacher. (Later, he too had a lapse into carnality but it was not prolonged as was Solomon's lapse). As a teenager, David faced the mighty Goliath. And in this confrontation, he illustrated the value of the combination of three qualities, faith in God, imagination and training (he was good with the sling while sheepherding). David repeatedly illustrated the value of one man full of courage, discretion, divine viewpoint and resourcefulness in a society; the value of just one such individual can be great, as our closing Proverb teaches.

On the other hand, antithetically and conversely, David understood that poor leadership, lacking divine viewpoint and courage, produces instability which in turn encourages depressions, gang rules, murders, wars and the like, with society experiencing a constant turmoil. And such conditions breed many evil leaders. Hence David highlights the potential value of the individual.

For the transgression of a land many are the princes (leaders of evil) *thereof, but by a man of understanding and knowledge, the state thereof shall be prolonged.*
Proverbs 28:2

Thus, wisdom is the principal thing, and with all thy getting, get understanding.

Bibliography

Bibles:

The Amplified Old Testament, Grand Rapids: Zondervan Publishing House, 1962.

The Berkeley Version of the Holy Bible in Modern English, Grand Rapids: Zondervan Publishing House, 1959.

The New Scofield Reference Bible, Authorized King James Version, New York; Oxford University Press, 1967.

Frost, Robert, *The Complete Poems of Robert Frost,* New York: Holt, Rinehart & Winston, 1967.

Glasser, William, M. D., *Reality Therapy: A New Approach to Psychiatry,* New York: Harper and Row, 1965.

Grant, Michael, *Myths of the Greeks and Romans,* New York: New American Library, Inc., 1962.

Henry, Matthew, *Matthew Henry's Commentary,* Vol. III, New York: Fleming H. Revell.

Moulton, James and Milligan, George, *Vocabulary of the Greek New Testament,* Grand Rapids, Michigan: Eerdmans, 1949.

Prescott, William Hickling, *History of the Reign of Ferdinand and and Isabella,* New York: The Heritage Press, 1962.

Taylor, Kenneth N., *Living Psalms and Proverbs,* Wheaton, Ill: Tyndale House Publishers, 1967.

Thieme, Robert B., Jr., *Proverbs Series,* 5139 W. Alabama St., Houston, Texas: Berachah Church, Tapes and Publications Department, 1966.

Trevelyan, G. M., *A Shortened History of England,* Baltimore, Maryland: Penguin Books, 1942.

Twining, Nathan F., *Neither Liberty Nor Safety: A Hard Look at U. S. Military Policy and Strategy,* New York: Holt, Rinehart & Winston, 1966.

Unger, Merrill F., *Unger's Bible Dictionary,* Chicago: Moody Press, 1960.

Young, Robert, *Young's Analytical Concordance to the Bible,* New York: Funk & Wagnalls, 1955.

GLOSSARY

Apostasy — Abandonment of one's faith, desertion of principles.

Carnality — Living under the control of the Old Sin Nature (See Chapter IX, "The Essence of the Soul"); being out of fellowship with God which means temporal spiritual death.

Details of Life — All those things in life which are temporal, whether they be necessities such as food, drink, or shelter, or luxuries such as hobbies, elegant clothing, or cars.

Divine Good — That good which is produced by God or that which is produced by the believer when he is under the control of the Holy Spirit.

Divine Viewpoint — Seeing the world as God sees it. This is possible for believers through the knowledge of Bible doctrine with which God reveals His character and thoughts.

Dying Grace — What God provides for the dying believer who is in fellowship and has some knowledge of Bible doctrine.

Dynamic Equation — FS + KD = DG, The filling of the spirit plus a knowledge of doctrine equals Divine Good. (See Chapter IX, "The Essence of the Soul")

Edification Complex — The reflection of the character of Christ and the glory of God in the soul of a believer. This consists of five facets: (1) Grace Orientation, (2) Capacity for Love, (3) Inner Happiness, (4) Spiritual Peace, (5) Mastery of the Details of Life. By reflecting Christ's character in our lives we can *edify* (to teach by example) those with whom we come in contact.

Fellowship (with God) — Being able to communicate with God. This is only possible when you have confessed your sins, I John 1:9.

Filling of the Spirit — Being under the control of the Holy Spirit, only possible when one is in fellowship with God. This state should result in the fruits of the Spirit, Galatians 5:22-23.

Frame of Reference — Having experiential knowledge in the heart on which to base decisions as new situations arise. This also results in an ability to understand more advanced doctrines.

Human Good — That which is produced from the area of strength in the Old Sin Nature by both believers and unbelievers. Although not categorically bad, yet human good has no positive merit in God's eyes.

Human Viewpoint — Seeing things without the benefit of knowing the "mind of Christ," hence exactly opposite from Divine Viewpoint, Isaiah 55:8,9.

Legalism — The delusion that taboos and self-denial are the means of pleasing God and becoming spiritual.

Mental Attitude Sin — Thought patterns which are contrary to God's revealed norms and standards, e.g., jealousy, envy, pride, and hatred. God judges internal sins of the mind just as harshly as overt sins.

Modus Operendi — Method of operation, here used to describe the divine techniques for living the Christian Life.

Old Sin Nature — That part of the human soul which is contrary to God's Holy nature, and which pervades all that the unregenerate unbeliever and carnal believer thinks and does. In times past this has been described by other phrases such as "Original Sin" or "The Sin of Adam."

Phase I — God's plan for the salvation of mankind from their sinful state. It was accomplished by Jesus Christ as He offered His perfect soul for the sins of man. It is appropriated by each man who believes and accepts this fact as his personal means of redemption.

Phase II — The Christian Way of Life with its principles and techniques designed to produce imitiation of God in the believer.

Phase III — Heaven or eternity; believer enters this phase at the point of physical death. It includes resurrection and eternal bliss with unlimited happiness.

Rapport Love — Total soul love between two persons who have compatability in the realm of Bible doctrine.

Rebound — Sin in the life of a believer destroys his fellowship with God. Rebound is the means of getting back into fellowship with God by confessing one's sins. I John 1:9, I Corinthians 11:31.

Repentance — Change of mental attitude from thinking and living contrary to God's laws and God's will.

Second Advent — Return of Jesus Christ to earth corporeally at some moment in the future (known only to God) to assume Lordship over all the earth.

Volition (Positive and Negative) — The facet of the human soul which is capable of obeying or disobeying God, commonly known as free will.